An Introduction to
Sixteenth-Century French Literature and Thought

NEW READINGS
Introductions to European Literature and Culture
Series Editor: Nicholas Hammond

Retelling the Tale:
An Introduction to French Medieval Literature
Simon Gaunt

An Introduction to Sixteenth-Century French Literature and Thought:
Other Times, Other Places
Neil Kenny

Creative Tensions:
An Introduction to Seventeenth-Century French Literature
Nicholas Hammond

The Search for Enlightenment:
An Introduction to Eighteenth-Century French Writing
John Leigh

An Introduction to Nineteenth-Century French Literature
Tim Farrant

An Introduction to Twentieth-Century French Literature
Victoria Best

French Cinema Since 1950: Personal Histories
Emma Wilson

The Challenges of Uncertainty:
An Introduction to Seventeenth-Century Spanish Literature
Jeremy Robbins

An Introduction to Twentieth-Century Italian Literature:
A Difficult Modernity
Robert S.C. Gordon

An Introduction to Sixteenth-Century French Literature and Thought: Other Times, Other Places

Neil Kenny

Duckworth

First published in 2008 by
Gerald Duckworth & Co. Ltd.
90-93 Cowcross Street, London EC1M 6BF
Tel: 020 7490 7300
Fax: 020 7490 0080
inquiries@duckworth-publishers.co.uk
www.ducknet.co.uk

A catalogue record for this book is available
from the British Library

ISBN 978 07156 3487 5

Typeset by e-type, Liverpool
Printed and bound in Great Britain by
MPG Books Limited, Bodmin, Cornwall

Contents

Acknowledgements

I am grateful to the Centre for Reformation and Renaissance Studies, University of Toronto, Canada, for a Visiting Fellowship during the tenure of which this book was begun. It draws on numerous studies, most of which it has not been possible to mention. Item 38 below, by Donald R. Kelley, inspired the structure of 'Five ways to become more human' in Chapter 3. The book's contents also owe much to what I have learned over the years from many students, and from my teaching colleagues Peter Bayley, Philip Ford, Liz Guild and Jill Jondorf. Moreover, Philip Ford, Liz Guild and the ever-patient series editor Nick Hammond read the typescript and improved it considerably through wise suggestions. Wendy Bennett, Alf Kenny and Yves Charles Morin kindly provided information on particular points. For moral support, I am grateful to Maureen and Alf Kenny, and to Leslie Topp.

Quotations from *The Complete Essays* by Michel de Montaigne, translated with an introduction and notes by M.A. Screech (Allen Lane: The Penguin Press, 1991, Penguin Classics, 1993, translation copyright M.A. Screech, 1987, 1991) are reproduced by permission of Penguin Books Ltd. Quotations from Donald Frame's translation of Rabelais are reproduced by permission of the University of California Press.

The book is dedicated to Leslie and Elizabeth.

Author's Note

Each chapter ends with one segment of a numbered list of editions and studies. The references in bold within the text are to that list. Italics within quotations are mine. Translations are mine unless otherwise indicated. Square brackets indicate my modification of a published translation. The modern studies suggested, with bias towards ones in English, are highly selective: many others would serve extremely well.

Texts

New editions of numerous French-language sixteenth-century works have been published recently, especially by Droz (www.droz.org) and Honoré Champion (www.honorechampion.com), although also in inexpensive formats by the Librairie Générale Française (Livre de Poche: www.livredepoche.com), Gallimard (www.gallimard.fr/) and others. Many works have been edited online and can be read on websites free of charge ('Epistemon') or they are accessible through a subscribing library or other institution ('FRANTEXT', 'ARTFL'). One can browse for free through the even wider selection of original sixteenth-century editions that have been digitized on the Bibliothèque Nationale de France website (www.bnf.fr/) (under 'Gallica').

Selected reading: introductory and reference works

Literature (and thought)

1. M. Simonin (ed.), *Dictionnaire des lettres françaises: Le XVIe siècle* (Paris, 2001). Very detailed.

2. D. Hollier (ed.), *A New History of French Literature* (Cambridge, 1989).

3. S. Kay, T. Cave and M. Bowie, *A Short History of French Literature* (Oxford, 2003).

4. F. Lestringant, J. Rieu and A. Tarrête, *Littérature française du XVIe siècle* (Paris, 2000).

Thought

5. B. Copenhaver and C. Schmitt, *Renaissance Philosophy* (Oxford and New York, 1992). Fairly advanced.

6. C. Schmitt, Q. Skinner, E. Kessler and J. Kraye (eds), *The Cambridge History of Renaissance Philosophy* (Cambridge, 1988). Advanced.

Society, politics, economy

7. R. Knecht, *The Rise and Fall of Renaissance France, 1483-1610* (London, 1996).

8. J. Salmon, *Society in Crisis: France in the Sixteenth Century* (London, 1975).

Language

9. W. Ayres-Bennett, *A History of the French Language Through Texts* (London and New York, 1996). The section 'Renaissance French' provides a good way into the language of the period.

10. A. Greimas and T. Keane, *Dictionnaire du moyen français: La Renaissance* (Paris, 1992). Dictionary of the language of the period.

Reigns

Louis XII	1498-1515
François Ier	1515-47
Henri II	1547-59
François II	1559-60
Charles IX	1560-74
Henri III	1574-89
Henri IV	1589-1610

1

Other Times, Other Places

Imagine someone who lives only in the here-and-now, their thoughts entirely devoted to their present moment and surroundings. Then contrast that person with an Italian thinker who, in a famous letter of 1513, described the evenings he spent in his study:

> on the threshold I take off my workday clothes, [...] and put on the garments of court and palace. Fitted out appropriately, I step inside the venerable courts of the ancients, where, solicitously received by them, [...] I am unashamed to converse with them and to question them about the motives for their actions, and they, out of their human kindness, answer me. And for four hours at a time I feel no boredom, I forget all my troubles, I do not dread poverty, and I am not terrified by death. I absorb myself into them completely. (13: p. 264)

Or, again, contrast the here-and-now person with a French poet who, in 1535, in the middle of an address to his king, described his thoughts as wandering off to a spiritual world beyond, ruled by a far greater king: 'Que dys je? Où suis je? O noble Roy Françoys, / Pardonne moy, car ailleurs je pensoys' ('What am I saying? Where am I? Forgive me, noble King François, for my thoughts were elsewhere'; 14: ii, p. 83). This propensity of the mind to stray from the here-and-now was summed up half a century later, with virtually the same words, by one of the greatest thinkers of all time: 'Nous pensons tousjours ailleurs' ('Our thoughts are always elsewhere'; 11: p. 49; 12: p. 939). And one of the remote places to which this Frenchman described his own mind as straying was the recently 'discovered' America: 'Notre monde vient d'en trouver un autre' ('Our world has just discovered another one'; **11**: p. 1423; **12**: p. 1029).

Educated sixteenth-century Europeans constantly travelled in their imaginations to other times and places. The quotations above illustrate the two most popular venues: the world of the ancient Greeks and Romans, imagined here, more than a millennium after its demise, by Niccolò Machiavelli; secondly, the Christian God's heavenly kingdom, imagined here by Clément Marot. Of the many other possible venues, another – a distant continent – is here conjured up by Michel de Montaigne. Imagining one's way beyond the here-and-now was hardly new. People had been mentally picturing the afterlife for centuries. But some imaginings were newer. In France, Greco-Roman antiquity was imagined with fresh intensity from about the late fifteenth century onwards. This also affected conceptions of the remote reaches of the cosmos. Meanwhile, Christopher Columbus and others transformed mental pictures of the Earth's far side.

Other times and places were also imagined by the largely illiterate peasants who, in France around 1500, accounted for 80-90 per cent of the population. (By 1570, the population reached a high of 19 or 20 million: **8**: pp. 30-2.) Moreover, although it is difficult to find out what less educated people thought, some historians have managed to reconstruct, for example, what a particular Italian miller imagined the remotest places of the cosmos to be like (**16**). Most people's here-and-now was, by modern Western standards, spatially and temporally limited, with average life expectancy in France in about 1500 being probably little more than 20 years, taking account of child mortality (**8**: p. 30). So the incentive to imagine times and places that preceded one's birth, followed one's death, or else remained invisible during one's life was perhaps at least as pressing for the poor as for the better-fed elite whose literary and intellectual culture this book introduces. But those elites had more time and resources to elaborate, research and describe for posterity their own imaginings of other times and places, such as ancient Greece and Rome (Chapters 2-3), God's kingdom (Chapter 4), the location of an absent loved one (Chapter 5), the recesses of nature, the cosmos and the future (Chapter 6) and far-off lands (Chapter 7).

Why were literature and thought so grounded in other times and places? To help people escape from present realities? In some cases, maybe, but more often, the point of connecting to other worlds – from antiquity to Heaven – was, paradoxically, to improve life in the present, whether that meant living more happily, virtuously, peacefully and meaningfully or else more wealthily, successfully, violently, with enhanced power and privilege. In either case, it was believed that detours into these other worlds tapped the deep roots – energizing or frightening – which anchored immediate experiences in larger realities, whether spiritual (Heaven), cosmic (connecting human nature to the planets), or historical (connecting sixteenth-century people to ancient 'pagans' or early Christians). Many writers stressed that an individual's life was the tip of an iceberg, and that we can only live well in the present if we connect with the spiritual, cosmic and historical vastness beyond. The attempt to connect could seem joyous or painful, passionate or perfunctory, successful or failed. In some cases it kept the other time or place distinct from the present, and in other cases, that very distinction became blurred: it became difficult for sixteenth-century Europeans to say what was 'then' as opposed to 'now', 'there' as opposed to 'here', 'them' as opposed to 'us'.

The iceberg of other times and places emerges constantly in sixteenth-century texts and artefacts, which can make first encounters with them disorienting. Why did Leonardo da Vinci and Michelangelo depict so many biblical and historical scenes? Why did Shakespeare set so many of his plays in foreign countries? Why did major French works that tackled contemporary social problems include so much on antiquity (François Rabelais, Montaigne) or the afterlife (Marguerite de Navarre, Agrippa D'Aubigné)? Such apparent detours may at first seem irksome. Yet what irks in texts is often the best starting point for approaching them, since therein lies their distinctiveness, their historical specificity, their challenge to modern expectations – in short, their own otherness when viewed from today.

The centrality of other times and places to much sixteenth-century French writing is evident even from a glance. Texts are often laced with snippets of other languages (especially Latin) and with words, names and allusions unfamiliar even to many contemporary readers. (By contrast, as the French seventeenth century progressed, such immediately visible traces of otherness or alterity were more often erased from the page, creating the smooth polished surface, the impression of homogeneity advocated by the 'neo-classical' aesthetics that became prominent in some quarters, alongside a new concern to standardize the French language.)

The imagining of other times and places was not purely mental: it was triggered by material objects. One kind was the printed or manuscript page. Others included: modern paintings and sculptures depicting the ancient world; new buildings that also evoked it; devotional objects, such as crucifixes, saints' relics; magical objects, such as amulets, which connected the wearer to parts of the cosmos; ancient Greek and especially Roman artefacts, such as statues, busts, ruins, stone coffins (*sarcophagi*), coins, medals, inscriptions; and trinkets and trophies from remote lands such as the Americas. Such was the evocative power invested in these catalyst objects that forgeries or counterfeits were sometimes made.

Language itself was another material medium widely considered capable of connecting people to other times and places. Educated people often believed that if they used certain styles of French or Latin, that would connect them either to the ancient Romans or else to the Bible. Indeed, in the case of Latin, this consideration led in fifteenth- and sixteenth-century Europe to the large-scale replacement of the living language of 'medieval Latin' by 'neo-Latin', which was more closely modelled on ancient Latin, especially as written from the first century BCE (or BC) to the mid-second century CE (or AD). This book, while focusing on French-language examples, also describes neo-Latin culture, since high culture in sixteenth-century France was essentially bilingual, as the next chapter will show.

Selected reading

Texts

11. Michel de Montaigne, *Les Essais*, ed. J. Céard and others (Paris, 2001).
12. ———, *The Complete Essays*, tr. M.A. Screech (London, 1993).
13. Niccolò Machiavelli, *Machiavelli and His Friends: Their Personal Correspondence*, tr. and ed. J. Atkinson and D. Sices (DeKalb, 1996). Includes Machiavelli's famous letter on visiting antiquity (pp. 262-5).
14. Clément Marot, *Oeuvres poétiques*, ed. G. Defaux, 2 vols (Paris, 1990).

Studies

15. N.Z. Davis, *Society and Culture in Early Modern France* (Stanford, 1975). Mainly on artisans, peasants, villagers and lower-class city-dwellers.
16. C. Ginzburg, *The Cheese and the Worms: The Cosmos of a Sixteenth-Century Miller*, tr. J. and A. Tedeschi (Baltimore, 1980).

2

The Ancient Past in the Present: Humanism (i)

2.1. Antiquity reborn?

High culture in sixteenth-century Christian France involved wide-spread imagining of ancient, mainly pre-Christian worlds, two of which loomed especially large: ancient Greece, from about the eighth century BCE up until and beyond its incorporation into the Roman Empire six centuries later; and ancient Rome, with its monarchy, then republic, then empire, from the eighth century BCE to the fifth century CE.

During the Middle Ages, those ancient worlds had not been forgotten in the West; far from it. Indeed, at certain times, concerted efforts were made to reanimate aspects of them. In particular, in the twelfth century, much Greco-Roman thought was revived thanks especially to the influence of Muslim Arabs such as Averroës (1126-98), the twelfth-century commentator on the ancient Greek philosopher Aristotle (384-322 BCE). Aristotle's extraordinarily wide-ranging philosophical system was given further life by St Thomas Aquinas (1225-74), who bolted it more tightly onto Christianity. Aquinas operated within a framework known as 'scholasticism' (on which more below). Scholasticism produced and transmitted knowledge in European universities from the twelfth century, and survived even into the seventeenth.

Moreover, especially from the twelfth century, students in Italy were trained in a set of techniques for writing documents and official letters in Latin. This *ars dictaminis* was modelled on aspects of ancient Roman rhetoric. It and other developments led, first in Italy, to what is discussed in this chapter – a much greater concern to recover certain aspects of antiquity in something approaching their original form, and to model one's own activity more closely on them.

There were some signs of this newly acute concern in Italy from the thirteenth century, but its outstanding early figure was Petrarch (Francesco Petrarca) (1304-74). In his time, many ancient writings were known in the West, but the Greek works among them only in Latin translation. Some ancient works existed only as incomplete fragments (*mutili*). Others were wholly or largely unknown but still existed physically, in this pre-print age, as one or more manuscript copies that lay more or less undisturbed in the library of some monastery or cathedral.

Petrarch launched a manuscript hunt, discovering some ancient Roman works. Even more were then discovered in the late fourteenth and early fifteenth century by (or at the instigation of) Coluccio Salutati, Poggio Bracciolini and others. For example, a search instigated by Salutati turned up in 1392 the informal letters that the orator and politician Cicero had written to his friends (*Ad familiares*); Bracciolini discovered in 1416 a complete version of Quintilian's treatise on rhetoric (previously known only as *mutili*) and in 1417 Lucretius's long philosophical poem *On the Nature of Things* (*De rerum natura*). The impact of each discovery rippled over the ensuing decades. For example, the *Ad familiares* was not widely known until a century later, in the 1490s, but it then became a schoolboy textbook throughout Europe for a few generations (**39**: p. 73).

The rediscovery of entirely or semi-forgotten ancient Roman writings was remarkably quick: by about 1430 the known corpus of such writings was almost what it is today. But an even greater cultural shock was underway: the recovery of ancient Greek writings in their original language.

Ancient Greek philosophy permeated the Christianized Aristotelianism that shaped the pedagogical system of scholasticism.

However, scholasticism knew Aristotle only through Latin translations. They had not even been made from the original Greek, but
rather (in the eleventh and twelfth centuries) from medieval Arabic
translations of Aristotle. The subsequent movement to recover
antiquity more accurately made it desirable to discover the original
Greek versions of Aristotle and of numerous others, many of whom
had long been unknown in Western Europe. Finding these texts was
one thing, understanding them was another, for knowledge of the
ancient Greek language had also become rare in the Latin West.
Tutors of ancient Greek became highly prized. The most influential
early tutor, Manuel Chrysoloras, arrived in Italy in 1397, having
come, like the others, from the Byzantine Empire, that is, from the
Eastern, Greek-speaking half of what had once been the Roman
Empire.

Soon, a cataclysmic event propelled more Greek and Greeks
westwards: in 1453, the Byzantine Empire fell, its capital
Constantinople (today's Istanbul) overrun by the Ottoman Turks
and incorporated into their expanding empire. Many Byzantine
scholars fled to Italy, bringing with them manuscripts of ancient
Greek works. By about 1500 almost all the ancient Greek works that
were still in existence had surfaced recently in Italy.

The scale of this recovery by the Latin West of ancient works that
it had mostly forgotten or never known was breathtaking. For
Roman antiquity, the recovery included whole authors (the historian Tacitus, the poets Lucretius, Catullus and Propertius), many
'new' works by already known authors (most famously Cicero), and
fuller versions of partly known works (by Quintilian and Livy). For
Greek antiquity, it included the vast majority of what we know
today: almost all the surviving poetry, history and oratory written
down by the ancient Greeks – from Homer's *Odyssey* and *Iliad* to the
histories of Thucydides and Herodotus, from the tragedies of
Sophocles and Aeschylus to the comedies of Aristophanes and
Lucian's satires – and vast swathes of philosophy and related writings, both whole authors (Plutarch), 'new' works by already-known
philosophers (all Plato's dialogues bar one; Aristotle's *Poetics*;

Archimedes) and by already-known medical writers (Hippocrates and Galen), as well as crucial accounts of various philosophies (neo-Platonism, Stoicism, Epicureanism and scepticism), and numerous early Christian writings in Greek. In addition, those ancient Greek works that had already been known – including most of Aristotle – were now transformed by becoming available in the original, as well as in new, more accurate Latin translations.

But what drove this recovery? Which aspects of antiquity were focused on? How, why and by whom?

The cultures of ancient Greece and Rome were vast. The new approach to them that gathered momentum in fourteenth- and early fifteenth-century Italy was selective. It focused mainly on reviving for modern uses what some ancient Romans had called the *studia humanitatis*, literally, 'pursuits of humanity' – the ancestor of our 'humanities'. The *studia humanitatis* comprised the language arts (grammar, rhetoric, dialectic and poetry), and also often history and moral philosophy. What did they have to do with 'humanity'? The answer was provided by the ancient who was *the* hero of the new movement: Cicero (106-143 BCE). According to Cicero, pursuing these subjects gives us a *humanitas* – a culture or education – that brings wisdom and realizes our human potential. We might therefore expect this core curriculum to consist of essential facts, of hard knowledge. Instead, it emphasized communication (the language arts) and ethics (moral philosophy). Knowing things, while important, was less so than communicating them powerfully and ethically. Indeed, knowledge was deemed useful only *if* it could be communicated thus.

The radical consequence – in conflict with existing scholastic education – was that the language arts (especially grammar and rhetoric) were master disciplines that should unlock all spheres of knowledge, not just, say, poetry, but also philosophy, theology and so on. And, sure enough, by 1500, the (now not so) new approach had been extended in this way. Geographically, the movement had spread beyond Italy to northern Europe. In France, it achieved increased acceptance especially from the late fifteenth century. It retained its core focus on the *studia humanitatis* throughout the sixteenth century, while also fanning out to all disciplines. Proponents of the new approach aimed to inculcate it in boys especially at the points when they learned basic and advanced skills of argument and expression – in what we would today call secondary education (in *collèges*) or at lower university level (in 'arts' or philosophy faculties). The three subjects taught at higher university level were theology, law and medicine. The new approach gradually infiltrated some medical and law faculties in France, but university theology remained largely resistant.

This movement had no single name, but one was invented retrospectively (in nineteenth-century Germany) – 'humanism', which echoes *humanitas* and vernacular usage, such as the fifteenth-century Italian word *umanista* for a teacher or student of the new-style syllabus. Modern scholars have debated what exactly humanism was. In recent decades, the notion (famously developed by Jacob Burckhardt in the nineteenth century) that humanism was a philosophy or set of values has been largely replaced (by Paul Kristeller and others) by a definition that centres on the revival of the *studia humanitatis*, on the cultivation of what were also called 'good letters' (*bonae litterae, bonnes lettres*), 'more humane letters' (*litterae humaniores*) and 'human arts' (*humanae artes*). This definition allows better for the enormous philosophical and cultural diversity of 'humanism' as it spread across Europe, being used differently in different contexts.

Humanists described their project as a restoration, a rebirth. From this terminology emerged, again in the nineteenth century, the phrase 'the Renaissance', which has often been used to denote not only humanism and its effect on art, architecture and much else, but also the whole period from (in the case of France) the late fifteenth to the early seventeenth century. But as some have long argued, using the phrase to denote the period rather than a movement can ignore the millions of French people who were largely excluded from this 'rebirth' of antiquity – not only the lower classes and the uneducated but also some of the old nobility and most women. Even among works written in the period, while a small number by women did, despite obstacles, engage with humanism, many by both women and men did not. If one restricts 'the Renaissance' to the period's high culture, the phrase still needs careful handling, since it can hide continuities with the immediately preceding centuries and so make us collude with the humanist propaganda claim that culture was vastly improved by the 'rebirth' of something lost. That would mean deciding that humanists were right and their enemies wrong.

Humanism attacked scholasticism. Although both were rooted in antiquity, they had contrasting attitudes towards it, and indeed towards historical time. Scholastics had long used Aristotle's writings as springboards from which to develop many philosophical, 'scientific' and theological doctrines, but without being strongly concerned to show where Aristotle's doctrines ended and theirs began, since what really mattered to them was rather whether the doctrines were universally true or not. And, apart from divine revelation, their main instrument for deciding this was dialectic or logic, that is, the art of reasoning by inference. By contrast, humanists wished to establish exactly what Aristotle – and other ancients – had written and meant. This involved what the humanists called philology, that is, using knowledge of ancient languages first to ascertain, from corrupt and conflicting manuscripts, exactly what the ancient author had originally written, and, secondly, to understand what his words meant, by relating them to his society, customs and beliefs. As Anthony Grafton puts it:

> The scholastics had read their texts as structures, systems of interlocking propositions that they tested for coherence as an engineer tests the load-bearing parts of a building. The humanists read theirs as clouded windows which proper treatment could restore to transparency, revealing the individuals who had written them. (**34**: p. 8)

This conflict was partly between a synchronic approach (treating past texts virtually as if they had been written at the same time) and a diachronic one (treating them as written at different points within the flow of human time). The humanists, partly diachronic in approach, historicized antiquity rather more. They emphasized that there had been a passage of time between antiquity and their own present. They called it a 'middle' time and a dark age, which had lasted – according to the humanist Guillaume Budé – between 1,000 and 1,200 years (**18**: p. 89); in other words from when the 'barbarian' invasions had ended the Romans' control of their empire up until Budé's own day. So humanist propaganda still shapes our own usual division of history – into antiquity, the Middle Ages and the Renaissance. That division is only now being threatened by a new label, 'early modern', which has an opposite bias, interpreting the sixteenth century as anticipating rather than restoring something. The humanists, by proclaiming a recent era's end and a remote era's return, denigrated as yesterday's men the scholastics who were in fact still very much alive and kicking. Humanist anti-scholastic satires – such as those by the greatest humanist, the Dutchman Desiderius Erasmus (*c.* 1466-1536) – were often so brilliant that even today it is difficult to avoid being manipulated by them, although research has long shown that scholasticism was extraordinarily dynamic, flexible and sophisticated. But the propaganda battle was uneven because it put the humanists on their favoured terrain. They were the communication specialists.

The most vivid French humanist propaganda was by Rabelais. His chronicles are among the greatest prose fiction ever produced. They recount the adventures of the giant Gargantua (*Gargantua,* 1534 or 1535), of his son Pantagruel (*Pantagruel,* 1532), of Pantagruel's friend Panurge as he tries to decide whether to marry (*Le Tiers Livre/ The Third Book,* 1546), and of this pair and friends as their search for an oracle (to resolve Panurge's dilemma) leads from one strange island to another (*Le Quart Livre/ The Fourth Book,* 1552). These generically hybrid narratives mix learning with scatology, philosophy with satire. In particular the earliest two attack the scholasticism of the Sorbonne (the University of Paris's theology faculty). The Sorbonne banned these and Rabelais's later chroni-

cles. Rabelais turns scholastics into snuffling, repulsive, logic-chop-
ping caricatures, such as Janotus de Bragmardo (*Gargantua*). By
contrast, a rebirth of antiquity is proclaimed, perhaps playfully, in,
for example, Gargantua's letter to Pantagruel. Whereas (writes
Gargantua) when I was young, 'Le temps était encore ténébreux et
sentant l'infélicité et calamité des Goths, qui avaient mis à destruction toute bonne littérature' ('The time was still dark, and smacking
of the infelicity of the Goths, who had brought all good [learning] to
destruction'), on the other hand,

> Maintenant toutes disciplines sont restituées, les langues instaurées:
> Grecque, sans laquelle c'est honte que une personne se die savant;
> Hébraïque, Chaldaïque, Latine. Les impressions tant élégantes et
> correctes en usance, qui ont été inventées de mon âge par inspiration
> divine [...] (**29**: p. 347)

> Now all branches of learning are reestablished, languages restored:
> Greek, without which it is shameful for a man to call himself learned;
> Hebrew, Chaldean, Latin; truly elegant and correct printings are now
> customary, which were invented in my time by divine inspiration
> [...] (**30**: p. 160)

But why did *Latin* need to be restored? Was it not already the
language of scholasticism? Yes, but scholastics, who put reason
before language, stretched Latin this way and that, inventing new
words to express their reasoning, whereas humanists contended
that the 'medieval Latin' (as we now call it) of scholastics and others
was barbarous. Humanists preferred to revive the Latin written by
the ancients, not any old ancients, but those who wrote what we
now call 'classical Latin', above all Cicero, whose 'periods' – or
groups of smooth, elegant, lengthy, balanced sentences – were
widely imitated in neo-Latin and indeed in French (including by
Rabelais in places). Indeed, early- and mid-sixteenth-century
France became the European focal point of Ciceronianism, a
radical campaign – derided by Erasmus – to ban from one's own

Latin any terms not used by Cicero. By the late sixteenth century, the choppier, rougher-textured Latin of Tacitus and Seneca was often preferred as an ancient model, in both French and neo-Latin, for example by Montaigne and the Flemish humanist Justus Lipsius respectively.

Gargantua's list of languages partly alludes to royal chairs in Greek and Hebrew which François Ier (lobbied by Budé) had endowed in 1530, soon adding a Latin chair (1534). These beginnings of what later became the Collège Royal were resisted by the Sorbonne.

For Gargantua, God sided with the humanists by giving them an incredible new weapon: printing. Block printing and even some movable type had long existed in China, but in about 1450, in Germany (Mainz), metallic movable type was invented by Johann Gutenberg and others. The technology spread quickly, reaching Paris in 1470 and Lyon in 1473. Suddenly one could mass-produce near-identical copies of the same work rather than having each copy laboriously made in manuscript by scribes. In calling printed texts 'correct', Gargantua echoes humanists' glee that they could now more easily establish corrected editions of ancient texts – knowing that they were discussing with each other the same version – before then distributing it in previously unimaginable numbers, alongside commentaries on it and translations of it, whether into Latin, French or other vernaculars. Humanism did not trigger the rise of print but was, like the Reformation, propelled by it.

Gargantua's association of old texts with new technology points to a tension within humanism. On the one hand, compared with scholasticism, humanism made the times and places of antiquity seem more remote. The more humanism discovered about them, the more different they seemed from the contemporary world – in religion, customs, language and so on. And yet, devoting such attention to antiquity made many humanists identify with it, want to imitate it in the anachronistic context of their own here-and-now. Humanism perhaps derived its dynamism from this tension between historicism and anachronism, between a perception of antiquity as being either long dead or else newly alive, either distinct from the present or else everywhere within it.

2.2. Why look back?

Paradoxically, it was mostly for present purposes that humanists imagined antiquity.

2.2.1. Humanism and the monarchy

In France, humanism often served the current interests of the monarchy, with which it forged a mutually advantageous alliance.

The sixteenth-century French monarchy, until the crisis into which the Wars of Religion plunged it from the 1560s to the 1590s, extended its power in several ways, ranging from territorial expansion to economic, legal and administrative reform. For example, a long series of efforts to acquire territory in the Italian peninsula began in 1494 when Charles VIII conquered (temporarily) the kingdom of Naples, inaugurating the so-called Italian Wars, which continued sporadically until 1559. Meanwhile, within the kingdom of France, especially under François Ier and Henri II, the monarchy greatly increased its control over many levels of secular administration, creating new offices (posts) that it filled with men owing allegiance to the King. This was also a fund-raising strategy, helping finance the Crown's expansionist military campaigns and other ventures, since to acquire these offices their holders had to purchase them. Moreover, many such office-holders lent money (*rentes*) to the Crown.

The monarchy also increased its control over ecclesiastical benefices (posts within the Church). Following an agreement between François Ier and Pope Leo X (the 1516 Concordat of Bologna), the King controversially gained from the Church the right to nominate much of the upper clergy in France (archbishops, bishops, abbots of monasteries and so on). These lucrative posts provided their holders with lands and income. Another change was the Court's expansion. This had started in about 1494, but under François Ier (1515-47) the fluctuating number of those at Court rose to anything up to 10,000. More of the nobility spent periods there, since that increased their chance of obtaining an office or pension.

Such contemporary developments could be promoted by the new kind of preoccupation with antiquity in many ways. First, humanism provided propaganda. In the Italian Wars (as in wars today), propaganda battles were as important as physical ones, since French kings needed the acquiescence of some Italian states in order to conquer others. So, for example, in 1511, Louis XII's tenuous hold on the Duchy of Milan was threatened by the Venetian Republic, the Pope and others. Potential allies such as the republic of Florence were much needed, and so a poet who was soon to be in the pay of the French King's wife (Anne de Bretagne) wrote a work that diplomatically presented Florence's Tuscan language as the cultural equal of French. The *Concorde des deux langages* (*Harmony Between Two Languages*) by Jean Lemaire de Belges did this by evoking a past partly styled by humanism: French and Tuscan both derive from Latin, 'mere de toute eloquence' ('mother of all eloquence'; **28**: p. 3); the *Concorde* includes imitation of Ovid, Virgil, Horace and Lucretius. But, unlike Rabelais, Budé and others, Lemaire de Belges does not claim a radical break with the more recent past, the Middle Ages. He was one of the late fifteenth- and early sixteenth-century poets that literary history has dubbed *rhétoriqueurs* or *grands rhétoriqueurs*. Most were, like Lemaire, commoners (as opposed to nobles). For their royal or aristocratic patrons they produced praise and propaganda characterized by extravagant word play.

Other writers promoted royal expansionism in Italy by evoking more aggressively a past defined by humanism. Joachim Du Bellay, in his *Deffence et illustration de la langue françoyse* (1549), argued that French should be enriched by writers imitating ancient Greek and Roman texts, just as Latin had been enriched by Cicero and others imitating Greek. Du Bellay concludes with a violent image: 'Là donq, Françoys, marchez couraigeusement vers cete superbe Cité

Romaine: et des serves Depouilles d'elle (comme vous avez fait plus d'une fois) ornez vos Temples, et Autelz' ('Now then, Frenchmen, march bravely toward that proud city of Rome. From its indentured remains, as you have done on more than one occasion, decorate your temples and altars'; 22: p. 179; 23: p. 91). He is recalling the brief occupation of Rome by the Gauls in 390 BCE. Here it is mainly a metaphor for the 'transfer of learning' (*translatio studii*) from ancient Rome to contemporary France. Many French humanists claimed that this transfer was underway. They thereby denied that contemporary Italy was the inheritor of ancient Rome. This took some denying, given that the Italians had geography on their side, that Tuscan was closer to Latin than French (in response to which Henri Estienne and others claimed that French partly originated in ancient Greek), and that the French envied the Italian cultural achievements of more recent centuries (Dante, Petrarch and Boccaccio) and of the present (in humanism, art and architecture). Moreover, Du Bellay was himself imitating a recent humanist dialogue in Italian (by Sperone Speroni, 1542) which made Tuscan the inheritor of classical Latin. But it was important for the French, in works like the *Deffence*, to turn their inferiority complex into one of superiority, partly because that provided cultural justification for the military 'transfer of empire' (*translatio imperii*) to France. Rome itself was not a military target, but northern Italy was. Indeed, only a few months earlier (1548) Henri II had paraded around French-controlled Turin.

Du Bellay's focus on antiquity also serves other royal policies. Like Gargantua, and unlike Lemaire, he joins the humanist clamour for a radical break with much of France's culture of recent centuries. That culture is old-hat, whereas, paradoxically, what is even older (antiquity) belongs to today:

Ly, donques, et rely premierement (ò Poëte futur), fueillete de Main nocturne, et journelle, les Exemplaires Grecz et Latins: puis me laisse toutes ces vieilles Poësies Françoyses aux Jeuz Floraux de Thoulouze, et au Puy de Rouan: comme Rondeaux, Ballades, Vyrelaiz, Chantz

Royaulx, Chansons, et autres telles episseries, qui corrumpent le goust de nostre Langue [...] (**22**: pp. 131-2)

Above all, then, future poet, read and re-read day and night your Greek and Latin [books]. Forget about all this old French poetry ~~~d out for such clubs as the Floral Games of Toulouse and the ~~~ of Rouen; for example, rondeaux, ballades, virelays, royal songs and other such trifles. These corrupt the taste of our ..] (**23**: p. 70)

genres denigrated here had been practised by poets *étoriqueurs* (dismissed by Du Bellay, except for ~~es at these regional poetry academies and ~littling of provincial poetry and language is a ~he administrative centralization undertaken (**22**: pp. 38-9). The *Deffence* ignores even the ~~ure of Lyon, which features only through poet Maurice Scève.

that humanists offered the monarchy (praise). As modern political parties ~o the monarchy tried to maintain ~ctly fostering certain images of ~e's greatest poets, Pierre de ~~ages at the courts of Henri II ~~al patrons. These poems ~ main ways. First, they ~ld to 'pagan' gods, for ~, his queen Catherine ~ France to Minerva. ~ent genres little prac-

~ for particular court ~ays passive, since it ~nd could be a ritual- ~xample, the eclogue (pastoral poem) 'Bergerie', which Ronsard wrote for the 1564 entertainments organized by Catherine de' Medici (by now ruling France as its regent), attributed the roles of the shepherds and shepherdesses to key young members of the royal household, including two future kings (Henri III and Henri IV). Written in what turned out to be only a lull in the early Wars of Religion, it seems to encourage the performers to behave peacefully in the real world b making them do so in a quasi-ancient pastoral world, modelled the bucolic (rural) poetry of Virgil (*Eclogues*) and Theocritus (31 pp. 143-73). Ronsard, as well as other humanist poets an scholars such as Jean Dorat, Scève, Barthélemy Aneau and R Garnier, also wrote poems and devised symbolic framewor the ceremonial entries that French kings made into cities, as for the celebratory publications that followed these occasion

French humanists claimed their antiquity-inspired produced the best praise since antiquity. Rhetoric of prais blame) was called epideictic or demonstrative. Dismissing royal propaganda, some writers told potential patrons paid eloquent chroniclers to praise them they would the imitating ancient (as opposed to medieval) patr addressing the young François Ier, argued that the Gre and others had – unlike François's predecessors – sens for their amazing deeds to be chronicled by approved added that the written memory of François Ier's d until the end of time thanks to the new medium of

Thirdly, some humanists offered legal backing tions. The monarchy's attempts to extend its p towards absolutism, which was then interrupte Religion before continuing in the seventeenth c under Louis XIV. The notion that the soverei stated most influentially by Jean Bodin in *République* (1576) – meant that he was above could change or ignore. The notion of ab Roman law – the sprawling body of laws Romano-Byzantine empire and that the Em codified (as the *Corpus iuris civilis*) in sixth-century Constantinople. The study of Roman law had been revived especially from the twelfth century onwards by scholastic commentators whom the humanists now denigrated, preferring to 'restore' it with their historicizing philology. The key figure was Guillaume Budé, the greatest early French humanist. His *Annotationes in Pandectas* (1508) were a vast commentary on the longest of Justinian's compilations (the *Digest* or *Pandects*). After Budé, France became the centre of legal humanism.

Budé's approach illustrates the humanist tension between historicism and anachronism. On the one hand, he emphasized that antiquity was very different from the present. On the other hand, he outlined some ways in which it could provide models for modern institutions and laws (this at a time when Roman law was still dominant in southern France). Humanist jurists of the University of Bourges (including Andrea Alciato and Jacques Cujas) pursued Budé's approach through the 'French method of teaching law' (*mos gallicus iuris docendi*): understanding Roman law in its historical contexts was a preliminary to re-applying now those aspects of it deemed just. For Budé, one such re-application was an absolutist theory of monarchy, drawn from the Roman law notion that the Emperor is unfettered by laws. Budé and others chose to identify this ruler (*princeps*) described by Roman law not with the modern-day Holy Roman Emperor (the secular equivalent of the Pope), who from 1519 was the Habsburg Charles V, but with the French King. His being 'absolute' meant having independence from Pope and Holy Roman Emperor.

For some, absolutism also meant that the King should be able to overrule if necessary the Parlement of Paris. In theory, the Parlement was part of the King's own council, but some of its magistrates took the 'constitutionalist' view that institutions should limit the King's power. In the climate of humanism, this conflict was played out on both sides through imaginary identifications with ancient institutions. Whereas François Ier saw himself as the Roman Emperor, the Parlement often saw itself as Rome's senate, which had flourished especially while Rome was a republic. No wonder Budé repudiated that analogy.

This shows that humanism did not *intrinsically* promote any single political philosophy. Whereas those humanists who supported French expansionism in Italy promoted war, Erasmus used humanism to promote peace. Whereas humanism often backed the monarchy, it also nourished radical Protestant theories of rebellion (especially from the 1570s). Indeed, one of the factors in the initial rise of humanism had been the opposite of absolutism: the determination of the oligarchs of northern Italian city-states to iden- tify with the Roman republic's senators and patricians as a way of claiming self-government and freedom from 'tyrants' (local dukes, the Pope and the Holy Roman Emperor). Salutati and Bracciolini were not *just* manuscript-hunters: both held the top post within the Florentine republic's bureaucracy, that of chancellor, as did Salutati's pupil, the celebrated humanist Leonardo Bruni.

Although French humanism operated in a different political climate from the republicanism of such 'civic humanism' (in Hans Baron's famous phrase), it too was largely geared towards active involvement in public life – called *negotium* ('work activity') by the Romans, as opposed to *otium* (roughly, 'leisure'). Hence the fourth way in which French humanism served the changing, monarchy- centred political order. Humanism provided training for the growing royal-sponsored bureaucracy, in Paris and the provinces. Courtiers, lawyers, magistrates, diplomats, personal secretaries, administrators, tax officials and other finance officers needed state- of-the-art communication skills, an ability to draft contracts and other documents, to arrange complex information attractively, to write or speak persuasively. Across Western Europe, state-of-the-art came to mean, paradoxically, ancient-style: in a quasi-Ciceronian (rather than medieval) Latin that bristled with classical allusions.

The *studia humanitatis* provided such training; scholasticism did not. Realizing this, with an eye to their sons' futures, numerous municipal councils founded a new breed of school, the *collège* or grammar school, staffed by humanist teachers (*régents*), and preparing boys of a certain social class for university study in law or medicine, for instance (**37**: ch. 7). *Collèges* threatened the near-monopoly previously enjoyed by the Church's long-standing cathedral schools.

2.2.2. The gentry, male and female

Which class benefited? The turn to antiquity was part of a social upheaval. The *collèges* helped the rise of a new class, labelled the gentry by George Huppert (upon whom the present section draws extensively [**37**]). Gentry males steered the burgeoning, royal-sponsored legal and financial bureaucracy. Paradoxically, their immersion in antiquity enabled them to do so.

Who were they? The gentry did not fit in with the traditional division of society into the three estates – clergy, nobility and the 'third estate' (which included the bourgeoisie and peasantry). On the one hand, the gentry were partly *roturiers*, that is, commoners – at least in the sense that they did not belong to the grand noble families that for centuries had possessed feudal fiefs or *seigneuries* and derived their income almost entirely from peasant cultivation of these lands; the gentry were not *gentilshommes de race*. On the other hand, nor were they straightforwardly bourgeois. Many of them had made their fortune in commerce, but then, wishing to 'live nobly', stopped being merchants, since trade was incompatible with nobility. Instead, they purchased fiefs. They also bought power in the form of offices, whether in the Church, in the financial administration or in the judiciary (for example, in one of the parlements, such as that of Paris – parlements were administrative centres as well as courts). Whether this made them truly noble was often controversial, but often, after a generation or two, the family generally passed for noble. Prestige and influence were not the only incentives: nobility brought tax exemption.

The *noblesse de race* or 'sword nobility' (*noblesse d'épée*) resented this usurpation of influence by the new *noblesse politique*, which was dominated by lawyers (and so became widely known in the seventeenth century as the 'gown nobility', the *noblesse de robe*). The old nobility's self-image was grounded in arms, in military prowess, and the gentry's in learning, in the *studia humanitatis*, which the *gentilshommes* often scorned.

The gentry's *studia humanitatis* not only benefited the monarchy but offered the gentry themselves money, glamour and power. The improved career opportunities even included poetry. In the late 1540s and early 1550s, two humanist preceptors, Jean Dorat and Marc-Antoine Muret, each only a commoner themselves, immersed in ancient poetry and (in Muret's case) in drama their socially superior pupils at the Paris humanist *collèges* of Coqueret and Boncourt respectively. A varying list of these pupils and other poets, seven at any given time, was subsequently labelled by Ronsard the 'Brigade' and then the 'Pléiade'. By this he meant that these were the seven stars of poetry's renewal via antiquity. Du Bellay's *Deffence* expressed aspirations more or less shared by them. The five who always figured in the list were Ronsard himself, Du Bellay, Jean-Antoine de Baïf, Étienne Jodelle and Pontus de Tyard. In contrast with the commoner-dominated *rhétoriqueurs*, the Brigade or Pléiade were mostly from the gentry or from the apparently older nobility, in which case they were from a minor branch and were younger sons (*cadets*) who did not inherit the family estate and so needed income. But even publishing poetry did not directly earn money. So what did they do?

In Du Bellay's case, although his noble cousins were high-ranking Crown officials, he was a *cadet* of a less illustrious branch and so his career involved being personal secretary to one of those cousins, the Cardinal Jean Du Bellay. Ronsard claimed, probably exaggeratedly, to be from an extremely ancient feudal family. For *cadets* like him and Du Bellay, a military career was standard, but Ronsard's half-deafness led instead to work as a courtier and, eventually, in return for services that included his poetry, to a string of clerical benefices for which, like many of the post-Concordat amateur clerics, he had qualified by becoming tonsured. (This involved in theory a commitment to celibacy but fell short of priesthood.) Further down the social spectrum from these two Dorat pupils was the Muret pupil Jodelle, whose lawyer family was probably bourgeois although he tried to hide this. He reinjected antiquity into drama, which earned him rapid success. His *Cléopâtre captive* was even performed before Henri II in 1553. But his death in poverty in 1573 shows the potential tenuousness of the 'letters'-based courtier career.

Most other writers discussed in this book were also humanist-educated gentry, whether Montaigne, Agrippa D'Aubigné or Guillaume de Saluste Du Bartas. But what about women?

Most women from the gentry were largely excluded from formal training in the *studia humanitatis*, as from the public careers to which that training led. Indeed, as Anthony Grafton and Lisa Jardine have shown in relation to fifteenth-century Italy, although a few women became humanists, they lacked vocational applicability for their skills, which were presented by male praise as extraordinary ornaments, cul-de-sacs of lady-like cultivation (**36**: ch. 2). In France, the ideal of the civilized, articulate, courtly woman was promoted by, for example, Antoine Héroet in his best-selling *Parfaite Amie* (*Perfect Friend/Lover*) of 1542 (**26**: pp. 5-70). Héroet was participating in a rhetorical for-or-against-women debate that had recently flared up among male authors, as an after-shock of the *querelle des femmes* initiated by Christine de Pizan in 1402. As Jane Stevenson has shown, some Frenchwomen, especially from the royalty and gentry, did gain extensive knowledge of antiquity and its languages through the *studia humanitatis*, usually with a father or tutor, sometimes more independently (**44**: pp. 177-98).

Moreover, they sometimes used this knowledge even in the public sphere. For example, Madeleine Neveu and Catherine Fradonnet, the Dames Des Roches, achieved this by operating as a mother-and-daughter unit. Madeleine, probably using the library of her lawyer second husband, acquired considerable historical knowledge of antiquity and educated her daughter. In their Poitiers home the women co-hosted a salon for humanists, poets, professors, lawyers and physicians. It soon became famous. They published three joint collections of their poetry and prose (1578, 1583 and 1586). Publishing – like speaking in the public sphere – was potentially damaging to women's honour and reputation, since it risked seeming to contravene at least one and possibly all three of the key virtues often enjoined on them: silence, chastity and obedience. Addressing men publicly, whether or not about love, could be considered unchaste. An unmarried woman could be particularly vulnerable to such a charge, even if her love poetry declared her independence from love and men, as did that of Catherine Des Roches. So her mother was her textual chaperone: 'Mamie, je sçay que la reverence, l'amour, et l'honéte pudeur, ne vous permetent étre sans moy au papier des Imprimeurs' ('My dear, I know that respect, love and chaste modesty prevent you from appearing on printers' paper without me'; **20**: p. 87).

Although as women the Des Roches were outside the charmed circle of patronage and office-holding, both used their knowledge of antiquity to compose panegryrics of the monarchy (on the occasion of the Court's stay in Poitiers in 1577 [**19**: pp. 31-3]). However, for them, in contrast with the Du Bellay of the *Deffence*, the ancient world nourished provincial as well as royal propaganda. Their poems often promoted Poitiers, even when it was in conflict with the monarchy, for example in its demand for a parlement that would give it independent jurisdiction (**20**: p.102). Another female visit from antiquity had been claimed by a more major provincial city, Lyon, when Louise Labé was presented as the Sappho of Lyon in her 1555 *Euvres*. The Greek poet Sappho, whose actual writings are little known, was being rediscovered as Labé wrote, and was one of the few possible ancient female poets with whom Labé could align herself, if a risky one given Sappho's lesbian eroticism.

With these rare cases, the capacity of humanist-revived antiquity to bestow visibility in the present was even more striking than with men, since with women it was not seconded by a bishopric or a diplomatic mission. And it was even more striking in Labé's case since she was bourgeoise (from a family of rope-makers), whereas the Des Roches were classic gentry. While the sources of their relatively modest income were compatible with 'living nobly', their poetry reveals their awareness that learning is mainly what provides them with noble credentials (**37**: p. 123). They make a familiar humanist claim that true nobility lies in merit not birth (**19**: pp. 48-9).

However, that claim did not usually apply equally to the two sexes. A woman steeped in antiquity, if not accused of sexual immorality, was likely to be dismissed instead as ridiculous, pedantic, unwomanly, unsound in her learning and not worth listening to. Marie de Gournay, humanist author, grammarian and translator – who described how she taught herself Latin against her mother's wishes, by comparing French translations with Latin originals (**25**: ii, p. 1862) – dissected these male reactions in her *Egalité des hommes et des femmes* and *Grief des dames* (respectively 1622 and 1626, but reworking 1590s publications).

For these writers and others, male and female, imagining antiquity was certainly much more than *just* a means to social or economic success. But we still have much to learn about the relation between French humanist-inspired writing and its authors' social class, despite pioneering research (**37**; **47**: ch. 2).

Selected reading

Texts

17. Jean Bodin, *Les Six Livres de la République (1583)*, ed. G. Mairet (Paris, 1993).
18. Guillaume Budé, *De l'institution du prince* (facsimile reprint, Farnborough, 1966). Budé's one work in French (1519) rather than Latin. Advising François Ier, it belongs to the 'mirror for princes' genre.
19. Madeleine Des Roches and Catherine Des Roches, *Les Oeuvres*, ed. A. Larsen (Geneva, 1993).
20. ———, *Les Secondes Oeuvres*, ed. A. Larsen (Geneva, 1998).
21. ———, *From Mother and Daughter*, tr. A. Larsen (Chicago and London, 2006). Anthology.

22. Joachim Du Bellay, *Deffence et illustration de la langue françoyse*, ed. J.-C. Monferran (Geneva, 2001).

23. ———, 'Defence and illustration of the French language', in *Poetry and Language in Sixteenth-Century France*, tr. L. Willett (Toronto, 2004).

24. Desiderius Erasmus, *The Erasmus Reader*, ed. E. Rummel (Toronto, 1990). Anthology of Erasmus's writings; in English.

25. Marie de Gournay, *Oeuvres complètes*, ed. J.-C. Arnould and others, 2 vols (Paris, 2002).

26. Antoine Héroet, *Oeuvres poétiques*, ed. F. Gohin (Paris, 1943).

27. Louise Labé, *Oeuvres complètes*, ed. F. Rigolot (Paris, 1986).

28. Jean Lemaire de Belges, *La Concorde des deux langages*, ed. J. Frappier (Paris, 1947).

29. François Rabelais, *Les Cinq Livres*, ed. J. Céard, G. Defaux and M. Simonin (Paris, 1994).

30. ———, *The Complete Works*, tr. D. Frame (Berkeley, 1991).

31. Pierre de Ronsard, *Oeuvres complètes*, 2 vols, ed. J. Céard, D. Ménager and M. Simonin (Paris, 1993 and 1994).

32. ———, *Selected Poems*, tr. M. Quainton and E. Vinestock (London, 2002).

Studies

Humanism and 'the Renaissance'

33. P. Burke, *The Renaissance* (Basingstoke, 1997). Accessible, introductory.

34. A. Grafton, *Defenders of the Text: The Traditions of Scholarship in an Age of Science, 1450-1800* (Cambridge, 1991).

35. ———, *Commerce with the Classics: Ancient Books and Renaissance Readers* (Ann Arbor, 1997). Includes a chapter on Budé.

36. A. Grafton and L. Jardine, *From Humanism to the Humanities: Education and the Liberal Arts in Fifteenth- and Sixteenth-Century Europe* (London, 1986).

37. G. Huppert, *Les Bourgeois Gentilshommes: An Essay on the*

Definition of Elites in Renaissance France (Chicago and London, 1977).

38. D.R. Kelley, *Renaissance Humanism* (Boston, 1991). Introductory.

39. J. Kraye (ed.), *The Cambridge Companion to Renaissance Humanism* (Cambridge, 1996). Mostly introductory.

40. R. Porter and M. Teich (eds), *The Renaissance in National Context* (Cambridge, 1992). Chapter on France by D.R. Kelley.

*Women (see also **36**: ch. 2)*

41. C. Bauschatz, 'To choose ink and pen: French Renaissance women's writing', in *A History of Women's Writing in France*, ed. S. Stephens (Cambridge, 2000), pp. 41-63. Introductory.

42. *Dictionnaire des femmes de l'Ancienne France.* Good information on sixteenth-century women writers (www.siefar.org/).

43. I. Maclean, *The Renaissance Notion of Woman: A Study in the Fortunes of Scholasticism and Medical Science in European Intellectual Life* (Cambridge, 1980). Advanced.

44. J. Stevenson, *Women Latin Poets: Language, Gender, and Authority, from Antiquity to the Eighteenth Century* (Oxford, 2005). Contains sections on France.

Printing

45. L. Febvre and H.-J. Martin, *The Coming of the Book: The Impact of Printing, 1450-1800*, tr. D. Gerard (London and New York, 1990). (*L'Apparition du livre*, 1958). A classic.

French writing

46. T. Cave, *The Cornucopian Text: Problems of Writing in the French Renaissance* (Oxford, 1979). Advanced. On Erasmian 'abundance' (*copia*) and its impact on vernacular writing, in particular Rabelais, Ronsard and Montaigne.

47. H. Weber, *La Création poétique au XVIe siècle en France de Maurice*

Scève à Agrippa D'Aubigné (Paris, 1956). Classic survey.

Rabelais (see also 46)

48. J. O'Brien (ed.), *The Cambridge Companion to Rabelais* (Cambridge, forthcoming).

49. M.A. Screech, *Rabelais* (London, 1979).

3

The Ancient Past in the Present:
Humanism (ii)

So humanist immersion in antiquity offered worldly rewards. But it was also supposed to fulfil human potential, essentially through the five subjects usually held to constitute the *studia humanitatis.*

3.1. Five ways to become more human

3.1.1. Grammar

Along with rhetoric, grammar was the bedrock of the humanists' attempt to reanimate antiquity. To them, grammar meant mostly the art of speaking and writing a Latin that was correct, elegant and modelled on the 'best' of the Roman authors. Teachers got pupils not only to learn morphological structures, but to read a wide range of ancient Latin texts and to learn excerpts by heart.

Beyond the classroom, among humanist scholars, grammar extended into philology, the contextualized history of language, pioneered by Lorenzo Valla (*c.* 1405-57), Angelo Poliziano (1454-94) and others. Inspired by them, Budé and Erasmus used philology to recover what ancient Greek texts had meant in their original contexts. Budé became a – perhaps *the* – leading Hellenist in Europe. Having read all the Greek texts he could get hold of, he published a pioneering analysis of the language's prose usage (*Commentarii linguae graecae,* 1529). French scholars' centrality within Greek philology culminated in a vast dictionary by Henri Estienne

(*Thesaurus linguae graecae*, 1572). Philology also extended to ancient Hebrew, where the key French figure was the polyglot Guillaume Postel. He delved beyond Greco-Roman traditions into Jewish and also Arabic ones. He represents the radical wing of a tendency known as syncretism. This was the view expressed by many early sixteenth-century humanists, including Erasmus and Rabelais, that the best of non-Christian wisdom over the ages could be harmonized with Christianity, since even some non-Christians had been unwitting recipients of God's revelation.

Others worried, however, that some of the ancient meanings unlocked by philology would make people heretical rather than wise. Even Budé insisted that ultimately ancient Greek culture was only valuable insofar as it could be transformed for Christian purposes (*De transitu Hellenismi ad Christianismum*, 1535). In 1514, opposition to the new style learning of old languages led to the Sorbonne's condemnation of the German humanist Johann Reuchlin for applying Hebrew philology to the Bible. In 1523, Rabelais, then a Franciscan monk, had his books confiscated as punishment for learning Greek.

Undeterred, like many humanists Rabelais then applied this grammatical and philological knowledge beyond the *studia humanitatis*, in his case to law and, in particular, medicine: among his first publications were editions in the original Greek of ancient medical texts by Hippocrates and Galen.

Rabelais's chronicles also reveal the new excitement surrounding grammar. For example, in the *Fourth Book*, the names of the numerous strange islands invite etymological decoding, whether from Greek (*Medamothi* = no place) or from Hebrew (*Ruach* = wind or spirit, for an island whose inhabitants survive on wind not food). Rabelais – or the publisher of the 1552 full version – keen to attract readers from beyond the small elite that was equipped to decode such neologisms (newly coined words), appended a glossary of obscure terms. Writing ancient languages into a modern one, Rabelais went in an opposite direction to humanist grammarians who either sought the ancient Greek or Hebrew roots of modern words or discredited false etymologies (a favourite pastime of Valla). Some even believed that Hebrew connected us to the reality of things themselves – after all, Hebrew was thought to be God's language, used by Adam to name the animals (Genesis 2:19-20). The *Fourth Book* suggests, perhaps equivocally, that proper names in particular might provide such a link to things.

The *Fourth Book*'s ultimate grammatical fiction is the episode of the frozen words (**29**: pp. 1151-9). On their ship, Pantagruel and friends hear amazing words and sounds ('voix et sons') at open sea, although they cannot see anyone. Like good humanists, they scour antiquity for possible explanations, which include the doctrine (attributed to Plato by Plutarch) that words can freeze. The ship's navigator then claims that the sounds and words are those of a battle that occurred there last winter. Now that spring is come, they are thawing.

Like grammarians, Rabelais here breaks up language into its basic building blocks. By explicitly distinguishing between sounds ('bou, bou, traccc, trac, trr, trr') and words, he draws not only on humanism but on scholastic grammatical theory (as he also does elsewhere). Rabelais materializes language: Pantagruel hauls onto the deck some of the shimmering, coloured, icy words. They are recent, a few months old, yet ancient too, since the names of the warring parties who shouted them ('les Arismapiens, et les Nephelibates') conjure up Jewish antiquity as well as one people described by the ancient Greek travel-writer Herodotus. So antiquity is strangely conflated with the present. The episode is a fantasy version of the problems facing humanist philologists: the travellers struggle to reconstruct a coherent link between past and present from the material word-fragments of an alien language that emerge uncontrollably, not even in sentences.

3.1.2. Rhetoric

Humanists claimed to revive ancient rhetoric not for antiquarian purposes, but to transform communication in the here-and-now. That might seem a tall order, since nowadays we often associate rhetoric with empty, insincere grandiloquence. Rhetoric has been in particular disrepute for about two centuries, since Romanticism. However, for over two millennia before then, rhetoric flourished (while also being attacked) in high culture in Greco-Roman antiquity, the Middle Ages and the early modern period. Rhetoric was generally defined as the art of persuasion and as eloquence. It did not come naturally but had to be taught. And the ancients had left a body of theory upon which that training was based for centuries.

How did humanists revive classical rhetoric? First, they relaunched some key ancient treatises on it. In the Middle Ages these had been known either relatively little or else only in a mutilated version. They included Quintilian's *Institutio oratoria*, Cicero's *Orator* and *De oratore*, and a Latin adaptation of the Greek composition exercises (*Progymnasmata*) by Aphthonius. In colleges and university arts faculties, the *De oratore* and *Progymnasmata* became rhetoric textbooks alongside longer-established ones (the *Ad Herennium* and Cicero's *De inventione*). Humanist scholarship also corrected in 1491 the longstanding erroneous attribution of the *Ad Herennium* to Cicero, and it reflected in new ways on Aristotle's already known *Rhetoric*.

Secondly, humanists made rhetoric more central than it was in scholasticism. In medieval pedagogy, rhetoric and grammar were often grouped together with dialectic (logic). These three comprised the trivium, which led notionally to the quadrivium (the four mathematical arts). Actual pedagogical practice far outgrew that scheme of the seven liberal arts. But one constant in scholasticism was the dominance of dialectic. In universities, establishing the truth by logical procedures was more important than communicating persuasively. Humanists inverted that hierarchy, thereby courting accusations that their elegant words lacked philosophical rigour. Some humanists (Valla and Rudolph Agricola [1443-85]) made influential attempts to inject some rigour by creating a new kind of argumentation or dialectic, which dealt in probabilities rather than in the certainties claimed by scholastic dialectic. This created a close association between rhetoric and this new humanist dialectic.

Humanists felt that rhetoric provided a much better preparation than logic for real-life situations. They venerated the ideal orator described by Cicero and Quintilian – someone who has acquired an 'encyclopaedic' training and culture (*humanitas*, Cicero's translation of the Greek *paideia*), not as an end in itself, but to enable him to intervene more effectively in public affairs. Ancient rhetoric had originated in law courts and politics. Ostensibly preoccupied with speaking, it had also always encompassed writing, and did so emphatically for humanists. Many followed Cicero in seeing the true orator (and writer) as someone who possesses not just skills and knowledge but also virtue. If the skills fall into the wrong hands they no longer produce good rhetoric. On the other hand, it was occasionally argued (in imitation of Plato) that rhetoric is inherently vicious, bent on deception.

In the *collèges*, once boys had acquired a certain level of Latin grammar, they learned rhetoric. The effects of this increased injection of antiquity into pedagogy are evident in virtually all texts quoted in the present book. With the odd exception (such as the master mariner Jacques Cartier's voyage accounts), each would have been considered rhetorical from start to finish: writers did not switch rhetoric on and off like a tap, saving it for purple passages.

Here is a generalized outline of the system of rhetoric. (Details varied between treatises.) 'Persuasion' had a broad sense. To persuade, the orator needed to: (i) teach listeners (*docere*) and give them proof (*probare*); (ii) delight them (*delectare*); and (iii) move or 'bend' them (*movere, flectere*). Cicero called these the three 'duties of the orator'.

Students learned that there were three branches of rhetoric. At any given moment, an orator or writer was always doing one or more of the following: (i) exhorting or dissuading (deliberative); (ii) accusing or defending (judicial or forensic); and (iii) praising or blaming (epideictic or demonstrative). Some genres of writing favoured a particular branch. For example, the poetry that flourished at court was largely epideictic. Advice books for princes, such as Budé's to François Ier (**18**), contained much deliberative rhetoric.

Composition involved five stages. The first was deciding what to say and argue. This was 'invention' (*inventio*). It did not mean inventing in the modern sense of coming up with something unique and original. Rather, it meant 'finding' one's material. And students were trained where to look: among a range of possible proofs and topics.

'Proof' was another broad concept. Three fundamental types of proof were identified (using Greek terms): ethos, pathos and logos. The first two did not even involve rational argument. Instead, ethos was what one said in order to present oneself as trustworthy and believable. (This was especially problematic for women writers, from Helisenne de Crenne to Marie de Gournay, since they had an uphill battle in establishing why anyone, especially men, should heed them.) Pathos was what one said to manipulate the audience's emotions. Logos was rational argument. Argument from example is among one of the various rational proofs that logos involved. From Budé to Rabelais, from Du Bellay to the Dames Des Roches, writers constantly defended a general argument by citing the example of an event or action from the past, especially antiquity. This exemplarity was an inductive (as opposed to deductive) kind of proof, since it progressed from the particular to the general.

Enormous help in 'finding' things to say was given by the system of 'topics'. These were like ready-made pigeonholes, pre-labelled and waiting to be filled. The writer slotted particular arguments, whether new or pre-existing, into the appropriate pigeonholes. 'Topic' means 'place' (Greek *topos*, Latin *locus*). Students generated rhetoric on a given theme – such as a person or an action – by running through a mental checklist of 'places' of argument. For example, what was the name of the person being praised or blamed? What was their nature? Their fortune? Their aims? Their actions? How did they live? And so on. Students carried around in their heads numerous topics that they could apply to any theme.

Students also memorized 'commonplaces' (*loci communes*). Usually, these were 'places' (or pigeonholes) that had already been filled, that is, eloquent sayings that fell under a general 'topic'.

According to Erasmus, '"Commonplaces" covers things like: It is very important what interests you develop as a boy; It matters what company you keep; His own is fair in each man's eyes; Offence is easy, reconciliation hard' (**54**: p. 637). For instance, the last of these might have come under a topic such as the virtue Justice. The quotation is from Erasmus's phenomenally successful textbook of Latin rhetoric (*De copia*, 1512 onwards), which was used throughout northern Europe in the first three quarters of the sixteenth century. The textbook is on the 'twofold abundance (*copia*) of things and words'. It advises students how to create their own personal notebook by jotting down, under general headings (topics), the examples, commonplaces and much else that they find in ancient authors as they read them. That raw material is then recycled in the students' own compositions. This notebook technique, and variations on it, lie behind the extravagant rhetoric of abundance (*copia*) that characterizes so much French vernacular writing of the period, with its long strings of examples, quotations and arguments (**46**).

This cultivation of copious 'invention' was one of the ways in which writers practised what the humanists called imitation. Proper imitation involved not slavishly copying ancient texts but rather incorporating them into one's own writing in an active, dynamic way. Recycling should create something new. Paradoxically, writers aimed to create texts that were profoundly of their own time by steeping them in antiquity. This pervasive presence of ancient texts in sixteenth-century ones is a flagrant example of what modern critical theory calls intertextuality. This concept came as a shock in the 1960s for anyone clinging to Romantic notions of originality. But sixteenth-century readers did not need Roland Barthes or Julia Kristeva to tell them that texts derive their meaning from the relationship to other texts. To them that was obvious.

So much for 'invention'. The second stage of rhetorical composition was 'arrangement' (*dispositio*). Having found things to say, one decided in what order to say them. Countless students learned, for example, the advice of the *Ad Herennium* (which concerns in particular judicial oratory). Begin with an arresting introduction (*exordium*); then outline the facts of your case (*narratio*); then explain which points you will argue (*divisio*); then give your arguments, to prove your points (*confirmatio*) and refute your opponents' (*confutatio*); and conclude rousingly (*peroratio*). In practice, as the *Ad Herennium* concedes, the optimum arrangement will vary. And sixteenth-century writers endlessly modified such classical *dispositio*, depending especially on the genre within which they wrote. For example, introducing his vast poem on the horrors of the Wars of Religion (*Les Tragiques*), D'Aubigné seems cavalier: 'Vous remarquerez aussy bien en la disposition la liberté des entrees avec exorde ou celles qu'on appelle abruptes' ('Similarly, you'll notice the *dispositio* is free, each book starting either with an *exordium* or in what people call an abrupt manner'; p. 229). Why? To rouse and shock readers.

Students were trained to save certain kinds of topics (*loci*) for the start of their piece, other kinds for the middle, and so on. Ethos-related topics belonged in particular to the *exordium*, when one tried to persuade people to read on. It helped at this point to flatter them discreetly – the topic of 'capturing goodwill' (*captatio benevolentiae*). Rabelais lovingly parodies this at the start of his prologue to *Gargantua*: 'Beuveurs tresillustres, & vous Verolés tresprecieux [...]' ('Most illustrious [drinkers], and you, most precious poxies [...]'; **30**: p. 3).

The third stage of rhetorical composition was style (*elocutio*). Having decided *what* to say and in what order, one now had to decide *how* to say it. Whereas invention concerned things (*res*), style concerned words (*verba*). It is the least strange stage to us nowadays, because, as the ancient system of rhetoric faded from education systems after Romanticism, rhetoric became largely reduced to style. So nowadays we often equate rhetoric mainly with metaphor, irony, rhetorical questions and so on. By contrast, in the sixteenth century, style was only one of five stages of composition.

Moreover, style was taught far more systematically than today. Students learned to use three types of style: plain or low (*genus humile*), middle (*genus medium* or *mediocre*) and grand (*genus grande* or *grave*). A composition alternated between these according to the key rhetorical principle of decorum: style should be appropriate to the theme, the audience, the speaker and the occasion. Generally, the more elevated the theme, the higher the style. The grand style was suited to moments where the speaker played most strongly on the audience's emotions (pathos). It typically involved particularly ornate or figurative language, often with Ciceronian hypotaxis, that is, extended, complex, balanced sentences, full of subordinate clauses. The grand style was therefore often appropriate for the peroration (conclusion), which was thin on information and rich in feeling – witness, for instance, Étienne de La Boétie's exhortation to readers to resist tyranny at the end of his *Discours de la servitude volontaire.* On the other hand, the plainer style was suited to conveying information and involved more parataxis, that is, simpler syntax with few subordinate clauses. Writers used the ancient trio of styles for new purposes of which ancients had not dreamed. For example, D'Aubigné claims that his *Tragiques* shifts from a low to a middle and then a grand style as it gradually moves from the corruption and atrocities of a Catholic-dominated world to the Protestant martyrs and their reward in Heaven (pp. 226-8).

Students learned an enormous arsenal of stylistic devices, usually known as figures. Viewed as deliberate departures from an imagined ordinary language, they were usually divided into figures of words and figures of thought:

(i) Most figures of words were ways of arranging language (called schemes). They included antithesis; the rhetorical question (*interrogatio*); the emotional exclamation (*exclamatio*); the apostrophe or address to an absent person or an abstraction; and the arrangement of verbal units in order of increasing importance (*gradatio*). Some schemes were techniques of repetition, such as anaphora – repeating the same word or phrase at the start of successive clauses or sentences. On the other hand, some figures of words were tropes rather than schemes. A trope gave a word a figurative meaning instead of its literal one. Examples included metaphor and metonymy.

(ii) Figures of thought tended to continue over a longer stretch of a composition. They often drew on several figures of words, but were considered to be devices of thought rather than of expression. Examples include *enargia* (a vivid description) and simile (an explicit comparison).

We have seen that imitation, that fundamental principle of humanist-inspired writing, involved invention. Imitation also involved style. Students were trained to fill their notebooks with ancient expressions as well as arguments. Erasmus's famous textbook on abundance (*copia*) advised about both (and blurred the distinction between them). By imitating such expressions and producing their own variations on them, students would find countless ways of saying the same thing – a crucial rhetorical technique known as amplification. Erasmus suggested 195 ways of saying 'Your letter pleased me mightily', such as 'The man who brought your letter brought a feast day' and 'Sugar is not sugar when set beside your letter' (**54**: p. 353). While the message remains unchanged, the impact varies with each change of wording. That is the whole point. However, if amplification is taken to an extreme, the message can get lost from sight among the verbal dynamism, which itself virtually becomes the whole point. This happens constantly in Rabelais, for example. For humanists, language was not only a tool for trying to get things done in the world; it could also be a dizzying world unto itself.

Whereas the first three stages of composition applied equally to oratory and writing, the remaining two stages applied in particular to oratory. The fourth was memory (*memoria*), that is, sophisticated techniques for remembering a speech. The fifth was delivery (*actio* or *pronuntiatio*) – using one's voice and body expressively.

Paradoxically, then, for humanists, communication methods had to be *very* old in order to be up-to-date and cutting-edge. To get this message across, humanist propaganda flaunted rhetoric. For example, Rabelais's fictional chronicles, as well as being written rhetoric from start to finish, showcase numerous oratorical set pieces performed by protagonists within the diegesis (narrative). In

Gargantua, when a humanist tutor (des Marays) presents one of his pupils (Eudemon) to the giant Grandgousier, Eudemon's oratory shows up the inadequacy of the non-rhetorical education received by Grandgousier's son Gargantua from his old-fashioned (that is, not-ancient-inspired) tutor Jobelin:

> Puis [des Marays] dit à Grandgousier: Voyez-vous ce jeune enfant? il n'a encore seize ans. Voyons, si bon vous semble, quelle différence y a entre le savoir de vos rêveurs mataeologiens du temps jadis, & les jeunes gens de maintenant.
>
> L'essai plut à Grandgousier, et commanda que le page proposât. Alors Eudemon, demandant congé de ce faire au dit viceroi son maître, le bonnet au poing, la face ouverte, la bouche vermeille, les yeux assurés, & le regard assis sus Gargantua, avecques modestie juvénile se tint sus ses pieds, et commencza le louer & glorifier, premièrement de sa vertus et bonnes moeurs, secondement de son savoir, tiercement de sa noblesse, quartement de sa beauté corporelle. Et pour le quint doucement l'exhortait à révérer son père en toute observance, lequel tant s'étudiait à bien le faire instruire, à la fin le priait à ce qu'il le voulsist retenir pour le moindre de ses serviteurs. Car autre don pour le présent ne requérait des cieux, sinon qu'il lui fût fait grâce de lui complaire en quelque service agréable. Et le tout fut par icelui proféré avecques gestes tant propres, prononciation tant distincte, voix tant éloquente et langage tant orné & bien Latin, que mieux ressemblait un Gracchus, un Cicéron ou un Emylius du temps passé qu'un jouvenceau de ce siècle.
>
> Mais toute la contenance de Gargantua fut qu'il se prit à pleurer comme une vache, et se cachait le visage de son bonnet. Et ne fut possible de tirer de lui une parole, non plus qu'un pet d'un âne mort. Dont son père fut tant courroucé, qu'il vouloit occire maître Jobelin. Mais le dit des Marays l'en garda par belle remontrance qu'il lui fit: en manière que fut son ire modérée. (p. 83)

Then [des Marais] said to Grandgousier: 'Do you see this young lad? He's not yet twelve; let's see, if you think fit, what a difference there is between the learning of your daydreaming theologians of the old days and the young folk of today.'

Grandgousier was pleased with the test, and he ordered the young page to speak his piece. Then Eudémon, asking permission to do so of the said viceroy, his master, cap in hand, open face, red mouth, eyes steadfast, and his gaze fixed on Gargantua with youthful modesty, got to his feet and began to praise him and exalt him, first for his virtues and good behaviour, secondly for his learning, thirdly for his nobility, fourthly for his bodily beauty, and, for the fifth part, gently exhorted him to revere his father in every observance, who was going to such lengths to have him well educated; finally he asked him to be willing to take him on as the least of his servants, for he asked for the present no other gift of the heavens than to be granted the favour of pleasing him by some agreeable service. He set forth all this with such appropriate gestures, such distinct [delivery], such an eloquent voice, and a speech so richly ornate and truly Latin, that he seemed more like a Gracchus, a Cicero, or an Emilius of bygone days than a youngster of this century.

On the contrary, Gargantua's whole reaction was that he started crying like a cow and hid his face in his bonnet, and it was not possible to draw a word out of him any more than a fart from a dead donkey. At which his father was so wrathful that he wanted and tried to kill Master Jobelin. But the said des Marais kept him from it by a fine remonstrance he made to him, so that his ire was moderated. (**30**: pp. 39-40)

Eudemon uses his voice and body expressively (*actio, pronuntiatio*). He shifts from epideictic rhetoric (praising Gargantua) to deliberative (exhorting Gargantua to respect his father). The praise is generated by standard 'topics' (virtue and behaviour; learning; nobility; and beauty). Eudemon's peroration aims to capture Gargantua's goodwill (*captatio benevolentiae*) by modestly asking only to serve. The *dispositio* is clear ('premièrement [...] secondement ...'). The Latin's style (*elocutio*) imitates that of Cicero and of two orators whom Cicero praised ('bien Latin'). Decorum is observed:

right from Eudemon's request for permission to begin, every detail is appropriate for the occasion of a 15-year-old, in the presence of his king (Grandgousier) and tutor, addressing a prince (Gargantua).

However, this is not a rhetoric textbook, but a narrative fiction. What gives this passage its power is not the rhetorical ideal's perfection (*eudaimonia* means happiness in Greek) but the comic clash between it and the unruly body. Perhaps the most important word is 'Mais [...]'. Eudemon's *humanitas* encounters Gargantua's animalism. Which wins out in such cases? The former, according to the distinguished critic M.A. Screech, who always finds an intact humanist message in Rabelais. The latter, according to the visionary theorist Mikhail Bakhtin, who mostly finds that Rabelais degrades high culture. A third possibility, developed by critics such as Terence Cave and André Tournon, is that the clash remains unresolved. Certainly, Rabelais uses Eudemon for humanist propaganda. And the message is reinforced when the humanist tutor persuades the enraged king not to kill his son's useless tutor. Rhetoric can produce civic peace by virtuously curbing our passions. But, if the joke is mainly on Gargantua, it is perhaps on Eudemon too. If the prince you are addressing is more like a cow or a donkey, then your own decorum and compliments risk seeming ridiculously misplaced rather than textbook-perfect. Eudemon's rhetoric is like an elusive jewel: beautiful, but beyond the reader's reach (its Latin words being reported only in indirect French speech), and out of synch with its surroundings. Somehow Eudemon both epitomizes the here-and-now ('les jeunes gens de maintenant') and yet also, like some time-travelling alien, resembles long-dead orators more than his own peers. Like many practitioners of humanist rhetoric, he is caught between worlds.

3.1.3. Poetry

The same can be said of humanist-inspired poets. Ronsard claimed to write French poetry that was radically fresh and innovative precisely because of how it imitated old texts:

> Errant par les champs de la Grace
> Qui peint mes vers de ses couleurs,
> Sur les bords Dirceans j'amasse
> L'eslite des plus belles fleurs,
> À fin qu'en pillant, je façonne   5
> D'une laborieuse main
> La rondeur de ceste couronne
> Trois fois torse d'un ply Thebain,
> Pour orner le haut de la gloire
> Du plus heureux mignon des Dieux,   10
> Qui çà bas ramena des Cieux
> Les filles qu'enfanta Memoire. [...] (**31**: i, pp. 626-7)

Wandering through the fields of the Grace who paints my poetry
with her colours, I gather together, on the Dircean banks, the
loveliest flowers, so that my industrious hand can fashion that
booty into this circular crown, triple-folded in Theban style,
which will adorn the supreme glory of the gods' favourite – he
who brought Memory's daughters back down here from the
heavens.

The landscape described here is remote in time and place from
sixteenth-century France. It is that of ancient Greece, and of gods
that Ronsard and his Christian contemporaries no longer believed
in, at least not straightforwardly. However, the point, emphasized
by the very first word, is that that landscape is being wandered
through by the French poet in the here-and-now of his imagination,
in the present tense of writing. With a characteristic Ronsardian
reflexive swagger, these lines describe less a past world than the
poet's present imitation of its poetry. The flowers he picks and inter-
weaves are ancient poetic texts – above all Pindar's odes, which
celebrate the banks of the spring called Dirce (l. 3), near Thebes, in
Boeotia. Allusiveness of this kind was one technique of poetic imitation. Another was close or distant paraphrase of the source –

compare 'les champs de la Grace' with Pindar's description of himself as ploughing the field of the Graces (*Pythian Odes*, VI, 1). Another was the imitation of formal structures – the triply folded wreath (l. 8) is the structure of a Pindaric ode, which consists of a triad (strophe, antistrophe and epode) repeated throughout the poem.

The quotation above is the first strophe of Ronsard's *Ode à Michel de l'Hospital.* It proclaims a new kind of poetry that imitates the odes of the previously neglected Pindar, as well as those of Horace. Yet, even they are less prominent than the persona of Ronsard himself, as the pronouns suggest. The 28-year-old's success in helping forge, through print and imitation, a new kind of *gentilhomme* career, that of Court poet, will also depend on another present-day protagonist whom Ronsard glorifies epideictically (ll. 9-10) and weaves into the past myth which this ode will narrate: the dedicatee Michel de l'Hospital, Chancellor of France, the King's greatest officer, and a supporter of humanism. The myth is of the birth of the nine Muses, daughters of Memory and Jupiter (l. 12), and this ode recounts how, having been banished by Ignorance, they return to France thanks to the Chancellor (l. 11).

The poem appeared in Ronsard's fifth book of *Odes* (1552; four had appeared in 1550). He exaggerates his innovation, wrongly claiming, in the collection's preface, to be the first to use the Greek term 'ode' (meaning 'song') in French. But these poems certainly did strike readers as new. Unlike the traditional 'fixed forms' we saw Du Bellay deriding (*rondeaux* and so on), the ode allowed poets the freedom to have greater variety of metre, by alternating line lengths (although all are octosyllabic – consisting of eight syllables – in the example quoted). The ode also allowed greater variety of rhyme, by limiting each rhyme to just two line endings, as in the above example, rather than having the same rhyme repeated several times, as was traditional. And Ronsard, emphasizing that these poems should be set to music, called them the first *lyric* poetry in French, since they imitated ancient Greek poetry sung to the lyre.

In fact, all of these features of the Ronsardian ode had recently been anticipated by other successful genres – Clément Marot's French-language paraphrases of the Psalms and Mellin de Saint-Gelais's songs (*chansons*). Nonetheless, Ronsard established the ode as a new poetic genre that could be devoted to a wide range of serious or light subjects. Imitations of Pindar could have been tedious, but Ronsard turned them into poetry that courtiers and others wanted to read.

For example, the above strophe has characteristic dynamism. Although it consists of a single sentence, its twelve lines contain eight verbs. The sentence begins not with a grammatical subject – whether noun or pronoun – but with a present participle. An impression of movement precedes the reader's awareness of who is moving. The representation of imitation as a dynamic *process* is enhanced when the verbs denoting it hang on line endings (ll. 3, 5), creating run-on lines that propel the reader forward instead of pausing. Yet Ronsard then uses the relationship between lexis (vocabulary) and metre (a line's length and rhythm) to slow everything down, mimicking the painstaking work of poetic composition. The insertion of 'laborieuse', which operates here as a five-syllable word, overwhelms and weighs down its octosyllabic environment (l. 6). The line has an expressively awkward stress pattern, which can be represented as 6:2 ('D'une laborieuse main'). Contrast the sense of expansiveness in the haunting first line. Its three key terms, rather than being stodgily contiguous, are ventilated by prepositions and articles ('Errant par les champs de la Grace'). And its rhythm is a skipping 2:3:3 ('Errant par les champs de la Grace').

The contrast between these two lines (1 and 6) is between what were, for Ronsard and the Pléiade, the two fundamentals of poetic composition: inspiration and labour, or nature and art. A poet should be both gifted and hard working. This poem's emphasis on both is manifesto-like. Inspiration is described here through a myth (that of the Muses). Indeed, throughout his poetry, Ronsard uses Greco-Roman myths to express fundamental human drives, experiences and fantasies. Myth and poetry are inseparable for the Pléiade, which considered that the most ancient and divinely inspired poets of all (such as Orpheus, Homer and Hesiod – who is also much imitated in the *Ode à Michel de l'Hospital*) expressed through myth the world's secrets (**31**: ii, p. 1175). The Pléiade often treated these secrets as an ancient theology (*prisca theologia*), deeper than the truths of history. Whereas historians merely chronicle what has happened, poets can describe more truly, through their fictions, the world's underlying structure – what Plato called the Ideas or Forms (**31**: ii, p. 1178).

In philosophical terms, the main framework that the Pléiade used to explain poetic inspiration was neo-Platonism, a tradition that developed within a Christian perspective the doctrines of Plato, especially in late antiquity and in Florence in the second half of the fifteenth century. The humanist Marsilio Ficino produced Latin translations of and commentaries on Plato that influenced the exorbitant claims made for poetry in France by the Pléiade and others. According to Ficino, building on Plato's *Io*, the Muses take hold of a poet's soul. This plunges him into a poetic frenzy (*fureur* in French). The four frenzies (prophetic, mystic, amorous and poetic) are routes by which an individual's soul can rise up towards higher spheres, attempting to join the World Soul – or rather to rejoin it, since our souls are fragments of World Soul that have become trapped in our bodies. The Pléiade, following Ficino's syncretism, saw this as a theory of how the Christian God inspires poets. The Ficinian theory is paraphrased in Pontus de Tyard's *Solitaire premier* (1552), for example.

Many seem to have believed that poetry could make one 'more human' in this way – although 'beliefs' can be complex and multi-layered. The theories certainly served the here-and-now interests of male gentry poets seeking patronage, as did their insistence that theirs was a specialist craft requiring an apprenticeship. Young men were unlikely to impress patrons merely by claiming to be inspired. So they turned in particular to the Roman poet Horace's *Ars poetica* as a model for writing guides to the hard labour and technical skills of versifying. There was a wave of vernacular treatises on poetics. Some (such as Du Bellay's *Deffence*) advised how to produce poetry in the broad sense of what we would now call 'literature', others (Thomas Sebillet, Jacques Peletier du Mans) in the narrow sense of verse – 'poetry' could mean either. An indication of the increased autonomy which poetry achieved among the *studia humanitatis* is that prose treatises on versifying were called *arts poétiques* from the late 1540s (echoing Horace's famous poem on poetry, the *Ars poetica*), whereas hitherto they had been 'second rhetorics' (**57**: p. 22). Poetry remained rhetorical, involving the first three stages of composition (invention, arrangement and style). But it was no longer just a sub-branch of rhetoric.

The ancient genre of the treatise on poetics was also imitated in Latin – for example, in Julius Caesar Scaliger's *Poetices libri septem*, 1561 – to guide neo-Latin writers. But vernacular *arts poétiques* conveyed principles of versification that were inevitably more modern, since they concerned a language, French, which functions differently from Latin. In Latin prosody, long and short syllables are grouped together as various types of feet, such as the dactyl (long, short, short). But French prosody treats each syllable as a foot. Most Pléiade poetry had either ten-syllable lines (decasyllabic) or twelve-syllable ones (alexandrines). The alexandrine became the default option from the mid-1550s. For example, Ronsard wrote various sonnet cycles, of which the first (*Amours*, 1552) is largely decasyllabic and the last (*Sonets pour Helene*, 1578) in alexandrines. There is usually a slight breathing pause (caesura) after the sixth foot (in alexandrines) or the fourth or sixth foot (in decasyllabic lines). The two parts into which the caesura breaks the line are hemistichs. In each there is usually a relatively self-contained phrase. The foot preceding the caesura normally receives major stress, as does a line's last foot. Some of the other feet receive minor stress. So, although French is not pronounced with as much emphasis as English, its poetry's rhythm too is created by stress, as we saw with the Ronsard example.

When scanning a French line, we need to be aware that a normally mute '-e' (or '-es' or '-ent') at the end of a word should in fact be slightly sounded if it is followed by a consonant within the same line, in which case it counts as a foot. So, in the Ronsard ode above, 'belles' counts as two feet (l. 4) whereas 'gloire' counts as one (l. 9). French stress can be subtle to non-French ears: it falls on the final syllable of a word, except if the word ends with a neutral '-e' that is sounded. Hence, in the Ronsard extract, 'laborieuse main'.

As for rhyme, its intensity is modulated by the number of basic units of sound (phonemes) involved. A single syllable may contain several phonemes. A rhyme based on just one phoneme is 'poor' (*pauvre*), as in lines 6 and 8 of the Ronsard strophe. A rhyme based on two phonemes is 'adequate' (*suffisant*), as in the rest of the Ronsard strophe, where, for example, 'Grace' and 'amasse' have [a:] and [s] in common. A rhyme involving three or more phonemes is 'rich' (*riche*) or 'acrobatic'. (The exact application of these terms can sometimes vary from one modern scholar to another.) The 'adequate' rhymes in this Ronsard example help produce a sound world that is musical, as befits the 'ode' (song), without, however, being so rich that the sound becomes as prominent as the sense. This contrasts with the ludic, acrobatic or even punning rhyme (*rime en équivoque*) used at times by the *rhétoriqueurs* and Clément Marot (for example **14**: i, p. 87).

Metre was just one of many aspects of ancient poetic genres to be modernized through imitation. Ancient genres now taken in new directions included not just the ode, but also the elegy (Ovid, Tibullus, Propertius and Catullus), the epigram (Martial), the epistle (Horace and Ovid), the epitaph (Catullus, Martial and the collection known as the *Greek Anthology*), the long philosophical poem (Lucretius, Aratus, Manilius and Oppian), the hymn (modelled by Ronsard on Callimachus and the Homeric and Orphic hymns, as well as on the recent neo-Latin poet Marullus), and, most prestigious of all, epic (Homer and Virgil).

Even more strikingly, the most widespread poetic genre (at least in love poetry) was not ancient at all: the sonnet. Fourteen lines long, it consisted of two groups of four lines (quatrains) followed by a group of six that was divided visually into two tercets. Initially imported from Italy, probably by Clément Marot in the late 1530s, it was associated by French poets above all with Petrarch's sonnets to Laura. Rare 'Moderns' such as he attained the status of venerable model normally reserved for the ancients. And yet, in Petrarch's case too, French imitation reworked the model drastically (see Chapter 5 below).

Similar tensions gave rise to another poetic genre (in that broad period sense of 'poetry') – French-language tragedy and comedy, imitating Greco-Roman models. Humanist-educated gentry started composing plays in French. They imitated in particular Roman tragedy (Seneca) and comedy (Plautus and Terence), but also Greek tragedy (Sophocles, Euripides and Aeschylus) and comedy (Aristophanes). They began heeding to some extent ancient dramatic theory (Horace, Donatus and Aristotle's *Poetics*, which was gradually popularized in France especially by Scaliger's treatise). They followed the example of humanist *régents*, such as Muret and the Scot George Buchanan, who had already begun using neo-Latin to imitate ancient tragedy in the 1540s.

Cléopâtre captive (*Cleopatra the Captive*, 1553) by Muret's pupil Jodelle, one of the Brigade, was the first French-language drama to intensively imitate Greek and Roman tragedy. (It did not have any single source-text.) There followed tragedies on ancient history or myth (such as Jacques Grévin's *Jules César* [1561] and Robert Garnier's *Hippolyte* [1575], *Marc Antoine* [1578] and *La Troade* [1579]). Imitation departed further from its classical models when some Greco-Roman-style plays recounted instead episodes from the Bible (Jean de La Taille's *Saül le Furieux* [1572] and Garnier's *Les Juifves* [1583]). Indeed, even Théodore de Bèze's earlier *Abraham sacrifiant* (1550) showed incipient humanist influence. With comedy, the adaptation of ancient models to the modern world was even more striking, since plays were set in present-day France (Jodelle, *Eugène* [1552]; Grévin, *Les Esbahis* [1561]; and Odet de Turnèbe, *Les Contens* [1584]).

Why these imitations of the plots, themes, phrasing and structure of ancient drama? Like the ode or elegy, humanist-inspired drama was used by young patronage-seeking gentry such as Jodelle to proclaim their innovative promotion of French culture and language. They too did so by rejecting home-grown genres:

> Quand aux Comedies, et Tragedies, si les Roys, et les Republiques les vouloint restituer en leur ancienne dignité, qu'ont usurpée les Farces, et Moralitez, je seroy' bien d'opinion, que tu t'y employasses, et si tu le veux faire pour l'ornement de ta Langue, tu sçais où tu en doibs trouver les Archetypes. (Du Bellay; **22**: pp. 137-8)

> As for comedies and tragedies, if Kings and States wished to restore them to their former dignity, usurped in the meantime by farces and morality plays, I would recommend that you devote your energy to them. If your objective is to enrich your native language, you know where to find your models. (**23**: p. 72)

Rejected by the gentry poets, these non-classical genres (to which one could add mystery plays) in fact appealed to a broad cross-section of society.

By contrast, humanist drama was addressed to the more educated. It was performed in particular at colleges and at Court, although also probably at provincial Court-like gatherings of gentry and aristocracy. Its interest lay less in suspense or psychology than in rhetoric. Protagonists use deliberative rhetoric to try and persuade their way out of political quandaries. They use demonstrative and epideictic rhetoric to amplify their emotional and ethical responses to extraordinary, gut-wrenching events that change the 'Fortune' of whole peoples. Love plays second fiddle to politics. As La Taille put it in a preface on tragedy:

> Son vray subject ne traicte que de piteuses ruines des grands Seigneurs, que des inconstances de Fortune, que bannissements, guerres, pestes, famines, captivitez, execrables cruautez des Tyrans: et bref, que larmes et miseres extremes, et non point de choses qui arrivent tous les jours naturellement et par raison commune, comme d'un qui mourroit de sa propre mort, d'un qui seroit tué de son

ennemy, ou d'un qui seroit condamné à mourir par les loix, et pour
ses demerites: car tout cela n'esmouveroit pas aisément, et à peine
m'arracheroit il une larme de l'oeil, veu que la vraye et seule intention d'une Tragedie est d'esmouvoir et de poindre merveilleusement
les affections d'un chascun, car il fault que le subject en soit si pitoy-
able et poignant de soy, qu'estant mesmes en bref et nument dit,
engendre en nous quelque passion [...] (**56**: pp. 19-20)

Its subject-matter should be nothing but wretched downfalls of great
lords, reversals of Fortune, exile, war, plague, famine, captivity, and
the appalling cruelty of tyrants – in short, nothing but tears and
extreme misery, rather than things which happen every day, naturally, and for ordinary reasons, such someone's death without foul
play, someone's murder by his enemy, or someone's sentencing to
death by the justice system for his crimes. For none of that would
move people readily or would make me shed much of a tear,
whereas a tragedy's sole true aim is to move and inflame everyone's
emotions astonishingly, and so its topic must inspire such pity and
distress in itself that, even when conveyed in bare terms, it sparks
some passion in us. [...]

Tragedy, especially in college settings, helped train students'
memoria and *pronuntiatio*. More generally, it taught actors and audiences how to use rhetoric and moral analysis in the real-life
situations which would confront them daily in their own future
gentry-type careers, as Crown officials, lawyers, magistrates and so
on. More broadly, tragedies touched audiences because they represented, mostly implicitly, the calamitous events of the Wars of
Religion (1562-98). For audiences of La Taille's *Saül le Furieux* or
Garnier's *Les Juifves*, the remote biblical events depicted onstage
were, on some level, the real-life tragedies happening in contemporary France. Garnier, the leading dramatist, was no ivory tower
observer of such events, but active as a magistrate (lawyer-cum-
politician), culminating in his 1586 appointment to the Great
Council, the juridical body closest to the King.

3.1.4. History

As we have seen, according to neo-Platonic theory, history lagged behind poetry in its capacity to make us 'more human'. However, most humanists considered one could not be wise without knowledge of history, especially ancient history. Indeed, for some in France, especially in the century's latter decades, history was the most important of the *studia humanitatis*.

Approaches to studying history included both poles of the characteristic humanist tension between anachronism and historicism. At one extreme, ancient times and places were studied less for their own sake than for their practical usefulness in the here-and-now. Humanists frequently authorized this approach by referring to an ancient *locus* (Cicero, *De oratore*, 2:36), which, for example, Budé here weaves into his advice book for François Ier:

> [...] Histoire: Laquelle Cicero pere d'Eloquence Latine a appellé tesmoignaige des temps, lumiere de Verité, vie de la memoire, maistresse de la vie humaine, messaigere de l'Antiquité. [...] A ce, que par les choses passées, on iuge & estime plus certainement les presentes, qu'on preueoye les futures, & qu'on en soit saisy contre l'inaduertence. (**18**: p. 43)

> [...] History, which Cicero, the father of Latin eloquence, called the witness to other periods, truth's light, memory's life, human life's mistress, antiquity's messenger. [...] It enables us to use past events to judge and evaluate present ones with greater certainty and to foresee future events, thereby saving us from imprudence.

To do all this, history must be written eloquently.

At the other extreme, ancient times and places were studied more for their own sake, on their own terms. The ancient model for this approach was Herodotus, the Greek chronicler of other cultures. But humanist philology and antiquarianism now took it further, as numerous documents were sifted through and critically compared. This approach placed less emphasis on writing history eloquently. Laying the foundations for the modern discipline of history, it was developed in France by Jean Bodin in his *Method for Facilitating Knowledge of History* (*Methodus ad facilem historiarum cognitionem*) (1566) and then by others such as Étienne Pasquier.

In practice, these two approaches usually sat together, if uneasily. The tension between anachronism and historicism was unresolved. Even the historicizing Bodin saw history as essentially serving the present:

> So history will show us fully not only the techniques that are necessary for living, but also what we should seek and shun, what is shameful and honorable, and which are the best forms of law, social organization, and happiness. (translated from **51**: p. 280)

Moral philosophy thus included politics as well as personal ethics. In this quotation, it virtually becomes a sub-branch of history, which teaches people how to live. We have already encountered the means by which history produces the 'precepts' mentioned here: examples. History supplies that storehouse of examples from which the orator draws some of his or her inductive proofs (under *inventio*). Here is Budé again:

> Car Prudence vient pour la plus part, par experience & obseruation des exemples du temps passé, dont Histoire (comme ie l'ay predict) est le Registre. (**18**: p. 66)

> For prudence mostly comes from the experience and observation of examples from the past; History is their record-keeper, as I said earlier.

'Prudence' and 'experience' have precise meanings. 'Prudence' is, according to Aristotle, one of the intellectual (as distinct from ethical) virtues. It is practical wisdom: the ability to decide on sound courses of action when confronted with real-life problems, such as those faced daily by magistrates and others. And, as Budé made clear in the previous quotation, prudence involves foresight (*prevoyance*), the ability to predict the outcome of such actions. Those examples, taken together, comprise 'experience' – the store of particular events from which general precepts can be drawn.

In addition, many tried to shape the present by using ancient history writers as models for writing the history of post-ancient times. In some cases, the aim was to legitimize, glorify and thereby strengthen the French monarchy. Paolo Emilio, although Italian, having been appointed royal historiographer by Charles VIII in 1497, published in 1516 the first books of a history of the French kings, which others continued throughout the century. Emilio imitated recent Italian humanist and propagandist historiographers as well as the Roman historian Livy. Persuading his readers through eloquence was more important to Emilio than analysing his sources critically.

In other cases, the aim was to write personal histories, memoirs. These were not personal in the modern sense of revealing some unique subjectivity. Rather, prominent men recounted their public deeds, military or political. They were broadly imitating the ancient genre of the heroic biography (the *vita*, which had, however, sometimes also covered private life, especially with Plutarch). When Marguerite de Valois – daughter of Henri II and Catherine de' Medici, and ex-wife of the man who had become Henri IV – wrote her own *Mémoires* in the late 1590s (published in 1628), she had few female models to imitate. So she too imitated the overwhelmingly masculine genre of the *vita*, but in new ways. For example, she prefaces her extraordinary list of childhood memories by paraphrasing a striking simile from the opening of Plutarch's life of Theseus:

Partant, comme les géographes nous décrivant la terre, quand ils sont arrivés au dernier terme de leur connaissance, disent au-delà, ce ne sont que déserts sablonneux, terres inhabitées, et mers non navigués, de même je dirai n'y avoir au-delà que le vague d'une première enfance, où nous vivons plutôt guidés par la Nature, à la façon des plantes et des animaux, que comme hommes régis et gouvernés par la Raison. (**58**: p. 73)

And so, just like geographers who, describing the Earth for us and having reached the limit of their knowledge, state that beyond that point lie only sandy deserts, uninhabitable lands, and uncharted oceans, so I will say that beyond this point lies only the abyss of early childhood, where we live guided by Nature, like plants and animals, more than as reason-governed humans.

Whereas for Plutarch the uncharted spaces are the many features of someone's life which elude his historian's grasp, for Marguerite de Valois they represent specifically her own pre-rational existence, what we might nowadays call the pre-conscious self. Her imitation of the Plutarch *locus* transforms it into one about the problem of self-analysis over time.

In other cases still, the historian had purposes so distinct from those of ancient models that modern models were presented as being more crucial. D'Aubigné's prose *Histoire universelle* (1616) had the confessional aim of promoting one branch of Christianity – Protestantism – recounting what happened to Protestants in Europe from 1550 to 1602. And yet, to create an impression of balance, it incorporates some of the lessons of the new, critical and objective-seeming humanist methods of historiography. It is exponents of them (Henri Lancelot Voisin de La Popelinière and Jacques-Auguste de Thou) whom D'Aubigné praises in his preface (**52**: i, p. 4).

3.1.5. Moral philosophy

Despite Bodin's implication that moral philosophy is a sub-discipline of history, it was usually the other way round. Humanists attached supreme importance to moral philosophy. It was subdivided into three branches, which taught people how to run society (politics), a family or household (economics) and themselves (ethics). Ethics promised answers to the question 'How should I live?'. Being Christian, humanists had answers unknown to their Greek and Roman heroes. But humanists still searched ancient moral writings for 'pagan' answers, sometimes in the hope that they could be harmonized with Christianity. This gave ancient ethics new meaning.

Humanism unsettled ethics by injecting into it more diverse ancient thought. Up until about the late fifteenth century, moral thinking in France had, like all philosophy, been dominated by scholasticism's Christianized Aristotelianism. But in the sixteenth century, the educated reading public could choose between Aristotelianism and Platonism, Stoicism, Epicureanism, Cynicism, scepticism and so on. These were not *just* moral philosophies. Except for Cynicism and scepticism (which both distrusted systems), each of these described the cosmos as a whole as well as telling people how to live. Many humanists became eclectic. Even if they favoured one ethical system, they still drew on others in certain situations, despite resultant contradictions.

Aristotelianism continued to be a dominant framework in ethics, whether through scholasticism or else through more direct humanist encounters with Aristotle (in the original Greek or in improved Latin translations), especially his *Nicomachean Ethics*. Like other moral philosophers, Aristotle posits a highest good – a supreme aim of life. For him this is happiness – by which he means living well, in a state of virtuous activity. Each virtue occupies a middle ground, a mean, between two vicious extremes, one of which is excessive and the other deficient. For example, the virtue of liberality (generosity) is the mean between the opposite vices of prodigality and stinginess.

As for the other ethical systems, we have already encountered Platonism in the Christianized versions known as neo-Platonism, with their understanding of an individual's moral life as the process by which his or her soul strives to rejoin the World Soul. For Plato (*c.* 427-347 BCE), the highest good is contemplation of the immaterial Forms or Ideas (such as Beauty, Truth, and above all the Good).

Stoicism was founded in ancient Greece by Zeno before thriving in Imperial Rome with Seneca, Epictetus and Marcus Aurelius.

Because the latter two wrote in Greek, they had been virtually unread in the Latin Middle Ages. For Stoics, the highest good is virtue, which they equate with happiness. They understand virtue to be an active effort of our higher faculties – reason and the will – which, if properly trained, can make us calm, 'apathetic' in the sense of being free from enslavement to our passions. Reason and the will can prevent us from directing hatred or fear at people, disasters or even our own health, which are all external to us, beyond our control, and so 'indifferent' (neither good nor bad in themselves). All we can control is our reaction to them, which is good or bad, virtuous or vicious.

Stoicism was Christianized by, for example, Justus Lipsius (whose 1584 treatise *On Constancy* [*De Constantia*] was well-known in France) and by the magistrate Guillaume du Vair, whose *Philosophie morale des Stoïques* (1585) came after his French translation of Epictetus's *Manual*. Some, such as the reformer Calvin, accused Stoics of an inflated view of our capacities, of wrongful reliance on human reason and will rather than on God. Nonetheless, Stoic advice to detach oneself mentally from the world appealed to many Christians. It helped many educated people through the suffering caused by the Wars of Religion. For example, Garnier, like other humanist tragic authors, drew heavily on Seneca's tragedies.

Epicureanism was even more resistant to Christianization. The Middle Ages knew Cicero's and Seneca's discussions of this philosophy. But it was unleashed in a more direct form by Bracciolini's 1417 discovery of Lucretius – the Roman poet who outlined the Greek thinker Epicurus's system – and by Ambroglio Traversari's much reprinted 1433 Latin translation of the *Lives and Opinions of Eminent Philosophers* (including Epicurus) by the ancient Greek Diogenes Laertius. For Epicurus, the highest good is pleasure. This is obtained not through hedonism, which leads to pain, but through moderation. This ethics, like Epicurus's denial of divine providence and of the soul's immortality, was difficult for most humanists to stomach. But Epicureanism became a disturbing, provocative presence in the ethical landscape.

The same is true of Cynicism, another Greek philosophy that had survived into ancient Rome. Key Cynics had included Antisthenes and Diogenes of Sinope. More austere than Epicureans, like the Stoics they argued that the highest good is virtue. Indeed, Stoicism first arose out of Cynicism. Both stressed the importance of asserting one's own autonomous will. But, unlike the Stoics, Cynics cultivated shocking lifestyles and gestures. Diogenes the Cynic lived in a tub and masturbated in public. Cynics put themselves at the margins of society in order to live closer to nature and avoid artificial, worldly comforts. They left no written philosophical system. Their ethics, transmitted by Plutarch and others in the fragmentary form of anecdotes and sayings, was again unleashed most spectacularly by Traversari's translation of Diogenes Laertius, which included a life of Diogenes the Cynic.

Another challenge to Christian morality came with scepticism. It was from 1562 in particular that this ancient Greek and Roman philosophy reached the forefront of educated people's consciousness in France. That year a Latin translation was published in Geneva by the humanist Henri Estiennne, of the *Outlines of Pyrrhonism* by the ancient Greek writer Sextus Empiricus. Some knowledge of scepticism had already spread from the fifteenth century via other ancient texts – in particular Cicero's *Academica* and Diogenes Laertius's life of Pyrrho.

Humanists were aware of the two sceptical traditions: pyrrhonism and Academic scepticism. The first went back to Pyrrho of Elis. It argued that everything that passes for knowledge is so uncertain that one should suspend judgement about it and refuse to hold any belief. Only this can bring the peace of mind (*ataraxia*) that is true happiness, the highest good. Even in ethics we have to suspend judgement, since we are unsure what is good and what bad. A later tradition was Academic scepticism, outlined by Cicero. It goes further than pyrrhonism by claiming that reliable knowledge is *definitely* impossible. But, having established this, it argues that some kinds of knowledge do at least have greater probability. It is thus less radical than pyrrhonism, which casts equal doubt on all knowledge.

The sceptical questioning of ethical (and other) systems was, unsurprisingly, attacked by many in Christian France, for instance by Ronsard's lawyer friend Guy de Bruès in his *Dialogues*, printed in 1557. But even Bruès's attack can be seen as ambivalent or open-ended. And some found a way of Christianizing scepticism, through an approach known as fideism. While accepting sceptical doubt about the products of human reason, they argued that it does not affect what we can know through faith (rather than reason) because God has revealed it to us through the Bible and other means.

For all humanist-inspired writers, the highest good was, quite simply, God. We could use labels to describe how they subordinated to that highest good the various goods of ancient ethics, but such labels are often inadequate. To take France's three greatest vernacular writers: we could call Ronsard a Christian neo-Platonist, Rabelais a Christian Stoic or Montaigne a Christian sceptic. But their texts tell a more interesting story, exploring ethical (and other) philosophies in imaginative, experimental ways. They might give undeniable weight to one philosophy, but still defend only some of its elements or leave its status unclear. They express both the excitement and the anxieties injected into ethics by humanism.

Rabelais's chronicles, for example, are eclectic ethical fictions. On the one hand, some of them represent as respectable a Christianized version of Stoic ethics. In the *Third Book* (1546), the giant Pantagruel often reacts with the calm detachment of a Stoic sage to his friend Panurge's attempts to decide whether to get married. When Panurge wears a strange outfit – featuring a cheap long robe and no codpiece or breeches – to show he wishes to mate, Pantagruel is unfazed. Moreover (he says), although such robes were once worn by certain heretics (an allusion to monks), he refuses even to condemn that aspect of their behaviour, because

> Chascun abonde en son sens: mesmement en choses foraines, externes et indifferentes, lesquelles de soy ne sont bonnes ou mauvaises, pource qu'elles ne sortent de nos coeurs et pensées, qui est l'officine de tout bien et tout mal: bien, si bonne est et par le esprit

munde reiglée l'affection; mal, si hors aequité par l'esprit maling est l'affection depravée. (**29**: p. 593)

Let every man be full of his own ideas, especially in matters alien, extraneous, and indifferent, which are in themselves neither good nor bad, because they do not issue from our hearts and thoughts, which are the workshop producing all good and all evil: good, if [the disposition is good and] ruled by the pure spirit; bad, if [the disposition is depraved and deprived of tranquility] by the evil spirit. [...] (**30**: p. 278)

Stoicism is here grafted onto Christianity: the opening phrase translates St Paul's Epistle to the Romans (14:5); vice comes from Satan. The rhetorical register helps us gauge the respectability with which Rabelais is endowing any philosophy. Here, the *elocutio* is all Ciceronian harmony and balance: hypotactic ('mesmement [...] lesquelles [...] pource qu' [...] qui est [...] si [...] si'), with elegant triplet ('foraines, externes et indifferentes') and doublets ('bonnes ou mauvaises', 'coeurs et pensées', 'tout bien et tout mal'), simple antitheses ('bonnes/mauvaises', 'bien/mal' repeated, 'esprit munde/esprit maling'), parallel clauses ('bien, si'/'mal, si'), and an elevated, abstract lexis that is part biblical (the opening phrase), part philosophical ('indifferentes', 'aequité').

However, in Rabelais, the fictional context complicates ethical theory. When Panurge then defends his outfit, although the defence is silly in its un-Stoic obsession with clothes, the silliness is perhaps made attractive by the ingenious zest with which Panurge's *inventio* harnesses *copia* to the material world. The monkish-habit look has (he claims) an occult property that is propitious to sex; the toga look, which he has modelled on Trajan's column and another Roman monument, is appropriate for peace-time activities (such as sex), whereas a codpiece is for protection in war. Stylistically, his speech contrasts sharply with Pantagruel's. It is all parataxis, word play (on different senses of 'bureau'/'bur'), and bodily, colloquial, rude terms: 'j'endesve, je deguene, je grezille d'estre marié et labourer en Diable bur dessus ma femme' ('I'm wild, I'm unsheathing, I'm sizzling to be married and go to work like a brown devil on my wife'; **30**: p. 278). Rabelais persistently interrupts high-register speech with its opposite in this way. Although Pantagruel occupies the ethical high ground, the low ground cannot be easily dismissed. Rabelais creates unresolved tensions between the two, between theory and practice, mind and body, high and low culture.

Moreover, the ethical theory thus enmeshed in Rabelais's fiction is itself eclectic, rather than all Stoic. Elsewhere, it is neo-Platonism that is given the 'respectable' treatment. It too features in Panurge's attempts to discover what will happen if he marries. He resorts to various methods of divination, consulting among others a madman and an elderly man nearing death. Pantagruel provides neo-Platonic explanations of why those two methods might work (*Third Book*, pp. 675-7, 779). Aristotelian ethics is also fictionalized. The comic pane-gyric of moderate behaviour (*mediocrité*) in the prologue to the *Fourth Book* has some of its roots in the scholastic doctrine of the virtuous mean. And Cynic ethics are visible especially in the prologue to the *Third Book*. The narrator there compares himself to Diogenes the Cynic, and his text to that philosopher's barrel, in a sustained and ambivalent exploration of the ethics of writing at a time of social upheaval. Rabelais's ethical explorations even include what Emmanuel Naya has shown to be the earliest substantial French-language engagement with pyrrhonism: another method of divination involves Panurge seeking pre-marriage counsel from a pyrrhonist philosopher, Trouillogan, who responds in apparently contradictory and bewilderingly non-committal terms.

Rabelais uses fiction to explore in open-ended, imaginative ways both the usefulness and uselessness, for the here-and-now, of ethical systems that originated in other times and places.

3.2. Don't look back? Michel de Montaigne (*Essais*)

Immersion in antiquity through the *studia humanitatis* was supposed to maximize human potential. But did it? Judged against the ideals of humanism, the life of Budé was extraordinarily successful (**35**: ch.

4). He was both a leading scholar and a holder of high public offices. His unrivalled knowledge of ancient culture informed his political, legal and administrative activity. But he was unusual in excelling in the spheres of both contemplation and action. Excelling in just one was a more common aim, but it involved dangers. Professional scholars risked immersing themselves so deeply in antiquity that they focused insufficiently on its potential applicability to (what we nowadays call) the 'real world'. On the other hand, officers, magistrates, finance officials, diplomats and even poets risked using their humanist education as a passport to money and power rather than to a virtuous civic life. These and other anxieties had long co-existed in humanism, but were more acute by the late sixteenth century, and came to a head in the work of Montaigne.

Montaigne moved away from civic action and towards contemplation when, in 1570, aged 37, he sold his office of magistrate in the Parlement of Bordeaux. He soon withdrew to the château and estate he had inherited from his father, devoting himself to reading, writing and estate management. Yet *negotium* still sometimes beckoned, in the shape of high-level diplomatic activity and two terms as Mayor of Bordeaux. He mainly read ancient works, pursuing what his humanist education at the Collège de Guyenne had begun. He began drafting reflections on what he read, grouping them in chapters which mainly had general headings such as 'Des menteurs' ('On liars'), 'Du dormir' ('On sleeping'), 'Des coutumes anciennes' ('On ancient customs') and 'Des prières' ('On prayers'). The result resembled a conventional genre called 'various readings' (*diverses leçons* or *variae lectiones*), which translated, paraphrased and amplified material from antiquity under thematic headings. His writing also had affinities with the genre of humanist commentary on ancient texts. As André Tournon has shown, it was also shaped by the long experience he had had of sifting through discrepant laws, commentaries on them and pieces of documentary evidence in the Bordeaux court responsible for particularly complex cases (**62**: pp. 19-22).

However, probably from the mid-1570s, he reached a realization that challenged humanism. Although he appeared to be writing about the ancients, and about liars, sleeping, and so on, he was in fact writing about himself – not just in the explicitly autobiographical passages, but everywhere. In 1580, the chapters were printed together, in two books of *Essais*. In the preface he wrote: 'Ainsi, Lecteur, je suis moi-même la matière de mon livre' ('And therefore, Reader, I myself am the [matter] of my book'; 'Au lecteur', **11**: p. 53; **12**: p. lvix). As he explains elsewhere, 'si j'étudie autre chose, c'est pour soudain le coucher sur moi, ou en moi, pour mieux dire' ('if I do study anything else, it is so as to apply it at once to myself, or more correctly, within myself'; ii.6, p. 601; **12**: p. 424). Such declarations were also instructions to readers, telling them to look out not for information about antiquity and choice phrases, not for *res* and *verba* to transfer to their commonplace books, but for the *way* in which Montaigne thinks and writes about such topics and applies them to himself.

There are two reasons why that *way* is so important. First, it is the closest Montaigne can come to discovering and also communicating how he thinks, reacts, even lives. On the whole, he does not see himself as first discovering things about himself and then communicating them. Rather, those discoveries are produced by the process of writing. When in 1588 he published an edition of the *Essais* that had numerous additions to the first two books, as well as a new third book, many of those additions were autobiographical or else reflected on what he had previously written, as if re-reading his work had triggered further insights into himself. The same is true of the further additions to all three books that he later inserted by hand into the margins of his copy of the 1588 edition (known as the *exemplaire de Bordeaux*).

The very title *Essais*, which no one had used before him, denoted this attempt to discover through writing. It denoted 'experiments' or 'tests' rather than what the now-familiar English term 'essay' means. In the following example, Montaigne describes trying to discover what Tacitus, the Roman historian, is like as a man. But beneath that 'test' lurks another:

J'ai principalement considéré son jugement, et n'en suis pas bien
éclairci partout. Comme ces mots de la lettre que Tibere vieil et
malade, envoyait au Sénat: Que vous écrirai-je messieurs, ou
comment vous écrirai-je, ou que ne vous écrirai-je point, en ce temps?
Les dieux, et les déesses me perdent pirement, que je ne me sens tous
les jours périr, si je le sais. Je n'aperçois pas pourquoi il les applique si
certainement, à un poignant remords qui tourmente la conscience de
Tibere: Au moins lorsque j'étais à même, je ne le vis point. Cela m'a
semblé aussi un peu lâche, qu'ayant eu à dire, qu'il avait exercé
certain honorable magistrat à Rome, il s'aille excusant que ce n'est
point par ostentation, qu'il l'a dit: Ce trait me semble bas de poil, pour
une âme de sa sorte: Car le n'oser parler rondement de soi, accuse
quelque faute de coeur: Un jugement roide et hautain, et qui juge
sainement, et sûrement: il use à toutes mains, des propres exemples,
ainsi que de chose étrangère: et témoigne franchement de lui, comme
de chose tierce: Il faut passer par-dessus ces règles populaires, de la
civilité, en faveur de la vérité, et de la liberté. J'ose non seulement
parler de moi, mais parler seulement de moi. Je fourvoie quand j'écris
d'autre chose, et me dérobe à mon sujet. (iii.8, pp. 1473-4)

What I have chiefly been considering is his judgement: I am not
entirely clear about it. For example, take those words from the letter
sent to the Senate by the aged ailing Tiberius: 'What, Sirs, should I
write to you, what indeed should I not write to you at this time? I
know that I am daily nearing death; may the gods and goddesses
make my end worse if I know what to write.' I cannot see why he
applies them with such certainty to a poignant remorse tormenting
Tiberius's conscience. Leastways when I came across them I saw no
such thing. It also seemed to me a bit weak of him when he was
obliged to mention that he had once held an honourable magistracy
in Rome to go on and explain that he was not referring to it in order
to boast about it. That line seemed rather shoddy to me for a soul
such as his: not to dare to talk roundly of yourself betrays a defect of
thought. A man of straight and elevated mind who judges surely and
soundly employs in all circumstances examples taken from himself as

well as from others, and frankly cites himself as witness as well as
third parties. We should jump over those plebeian rules of etiquette
in favour of truth and freedom. I not only dare to talk about myself
but to talk of nothing but myself. I am wandering off the point when
I write of anything else, cheating my subject of *me*. (12: p. 1067)

Montaigne describes himself as reading Tacitus less for information
about an episode in Roman history – Emperor Tiberius's letter to
the Senate defending Cotta Messalinus (*Annals*, 6:6) – than to
examine Tacitus's judgement – a faculty of moral discrimination, to
which Montaigne attaches enormous importance. Beneath this 'test'
of Tacitus's judgement lies one of Montaigne's own, for Montaigne
in turn exercises his own judgement in judging Tacitus's.

Generations of boys in humanist colleges were taught to hone
their judgement in this kind of way. Yet Montaigne goes further.
Rather than building up a coherent picture of Tacitus the man, he
highlights that man's inconsistency. He is intrigued by exceptions
to the rule of Tacitus's generally sound judgement, but he offers no
explanation for them. Indeed, Montaigne devotes another chapter
(ii.1) to such inconsistencies in people's behaviour. There, as here,
by simply juxtaposing two aspects of someone, without resolving
the discrepancy between them, he suspends his own judgement
about the person's character ('et n'en suis pas bien éclairci
partout'). This tactic is pyrrhonist. Having read Estienne's translation of Sextus Empiricus, probably in the mid-1570s, Montaigne
constantly juxtaposes not only aspects of somebody's behaviour
but also discordant opinions – held by ancients, himself and others
– about anything. Although he engages both sympathetically and
critically with other ancient philosophies, especially on ethics
(Stoicism, Epicureanism, even Cynicism), arguably he gives
pyrrhonist scepticism special status by letting it embrace his
engagement with those other philosophies. For example, in the
most explicitly pyrrhonist chapter of all, he argues that it is impossible to adjudicate between the highest goods posited by such
philosophies (ii.12, pp. 895-6).

On the other hand, the label 'Montaigne the sceptic' is too generic to be adequate. For example, it leaves open the still controversial question of the relationship between pyrrhonism and Catholicism in the *Essais*. The label also fails to describe the Montaigne-specific practice of writing that he develops out of pyrrhonism. In recording the inconsistencies of his own judgements, he relates them to the material circumstances in which he made them, including his age, his mood and the state of his body. Judgements are all relative to time and place. That is why he takes care to describe not what he *thinks* – once and for all – of Tacitus's judgement of Tiberius, but what he *thought* of it when he last read it ('Au moins lorsque j'étais à même').

So, although Montaigne places new emphasis on the here-and-now of the living, first-person judge as the sole destination of the humanist journey through the remote times and places of antiquity, in fact that here-and-now is itself elusive. As soon as a judgement is formulated, it is yet another object to be judged, in the flow of time. In painting myself (he writes),

> Je ne peins pas l'être, je peins le passage: non un passage d'âge en autre, ou comme dit le peuple, de sept en sept ans, mais de jour en jour, de minute en minute. Il faut accommoder mon histoire à l'heure. Je pourrai tantôt changer, non de fortune seulement, mais aussi d'intention: C'est un contrôle de divers et muables accidents, et d'imaginations irrésolues, et quand il y échoit, contraires: soit que je sois autre moi-même, soit que je saisisse les sujets, par autres circonstances, et considérations. (iii.2, p. 1256)

> I am not portraying being but becoming: not the passage from one age to another (or, as the folk put it, from one seven-year period to the next) but from day to day, from minute to minute. I must adapt this account of myself to the passing hour. I shall perhaps change soon, not [only in my external circumstances but also in my thoughts]. This is a register of varied and changing occurrences, of ideas which are unresolved and, when needs be, contradictory, either

> because I myself have become different or because I grasp hold of
> different attributes or aspects of my subjects. (**12**: pp. 907-8)

Whereas for most Catholic male gentry, the realm of 'otherness' was
that of ancients, foreigners, women and so on, the last sentence here
makes explicit that for Montaigne it is also within himself.
Otherness (alterity) is everywhere in the present as well as in the
past. Or, more accurately, alterity means that there is no absolute
present, however hard Montaigne tries to record his present
consciousness or (especially in iii.13) the present state of his body.

That brings us to the second reason why Montaigne instructs
readers to look for *how* he thinks and writes about something. If
beneath Montaigne's 'test' (*essai*) of Tacitus lies a test of himself, then
beneath that there lies a third: an invitation for the reader to 'test'
him or herself. Like Montaigne's self-portraying, this invitation is
largely implicit. Yet he occasionally spells it out. Of his thematic
material, he writes:

> Pour en ranger davantage, je n'en entasse que les têtes. Que j'y attache
> leur suite, je multiplierai plusieurs fois ce volume. Et combien y ai-je
> épandu d'histoires, qui ne disent mot, lesquelles qui voudra éplucher
> un peu curieusement, en produira infinis Essais? (i.40, p. 389)

> To [arrange more of it], I merely pile up the heads of argument: if I
> were to develop them as well I would increase the size of this tome
> several times over. And how many tacit *exempla* have I scattered over
> my pages which could all give rise to essays without number if
> anyone were to pluck them apart [with some care]. (**12**: p. 281)

Here the invitation is limited to the many ancient (and other) opinions and anecdotes which Montaigne reports without making clear
what he thinks of them, leaving them in a pyrrhonist limbo. But the
doubt that ultimately surrounds even those judgements that he *does*
formulate about other opinions and anecdotes constantly challenges
the reader to discover what *he or she* thinks of them. Indeed, ask any

thoughtful reader of Montaigne, and that is the effect that the work has on them. Montaigne has kept that much within his control. However, what opinions readers do actually reach, and whether they take up his challenge to doubt them, are beyond his control. In this sense, Montaigne accepts that his readers are 'other' to him. As the tenses in the quotation indicate, he acknowledges the existence of future as well as past and present alterity.

This questions the goal of ancient and humanist ethics, which was to teach people how to live: 'Les autres forment l'homme, je le récite: et en représente un particulier, bien mal formé' ('Others form Man; I give an account of Man and sketch a picture of a particular one of them who is very badly formed'; iii.2, p. 1255; **12**: p. 907). Certainly, Montaigne does dispense ethical advice, including the exhortation to try and discover one's own singularities. But he also encourages readers to treat all he writes – including his advice – critically, and as belonging, at a deep level, to his own self-portraying.

This questioning of moral philosophy undermines humanist application of history's supposed lessons to present-day situations. The store of examples drawn on by humanist *inventio* loses some authority: 'La vie de Caesar n'a point plus d'exemple, que la nôtre pour nous' ('Even the life of Caesar is less exemplary for us than our own'; iii.13, p. 1671; **12**: p. 1218). Tensions within the system of exemplarity had long been evident. But Montaigne strains them to breaking point by arguing – especially at the start of this final chapter, on 'experience' – that human singularity cannot be moulded to fit universal ethical examples, just as legal and medical cases are irreducible to positive laws or medical theory. In his philosophical terminology, particulars always outstrip universals. But that is not the final word. Montaigne always leaves space for an actual or potential counter-balancing argument. Centrifugal singularity and alterity are sometimes countered by a centripetal force, both within each individual (since each tends towards a distinctive 'form': iii.2, p. 1266) and within the species (since collectively we tend towards a common 'form': iii.2, p. 1256).

Doubt therefore undermines not only exemplarity but the virtue of prudence which humanists believed it to nourish. Montaigne is less optimistic that prudence can devise, through deliberative rhetoric, courses of public action that are likely to succeed. Without abandoning prudence, he draws on Stoicism to emphasize the unforeseeable more than the foreseeable:

Ne pouvant régler les événements, je me règle moi-même: et m'applique à eux, s'ils ne s'appliquent à moi. Je n'ai guère d'art pour savoir gauchir la fortune, et lui échapper, ou la forcer; et pour dresser et conduire par prudence les choses à mon point. (ii.17, p. 994)

Not being able to control events I control myself: if they will not adapt to me then I adapt to them. I have hardly any of the art of knowing how to cheat Fortune, of escaping her or compelling her, nor of dressing and guiding affairs to my purpose by [prudence]. (**12**: p. 732)

He denounces the memorizing of examples and excerpts in humanist pedagogy. Undigested, they render the student's judgement less rather than more flexible in responding to situations and in drawing lessons from their own experience (i.25-6). Philology often leads to vainglorious pedantry (i.39, pp. 373-4). Rhetoric often becomes a deceitful display of power rather than a stab at the truth (i.9, i.51, iii.8).

None of these attacks on the *studia humanitatis* were entirely new. Some even echoed ancient ones. But they had perhaps never been so searching. And they expressed increased pessimism among some gentry about the humanist project of reviving the past in the present. Humanism continued. Indeed, aspects of it live on today in its descendant, the humanities (**36**). Antiquity remained the main landscape in which Montaigne roamed mentally. But he now valued it especially for what his awkward, unresolved, inspiring or alienating encounters there taught him about his own distinctiveness. For some in the next generation, such as the philosopher René

Descartes, this helped beg a question that was unthinkable even for Montaigne: is that landscape really indispensable? Modernity was beckoning.

Selected reading

Texts

50. *Anthologie de la poésie française du XVIe siècle*, ed. J. Céard (Paris, 2005).

51. Jean Bodin, *Oeuvres philosophiques*, ed. and tr. P. Mesnard (Paris, 1951). Includes Latin original and French translation of the *Methodus ad facilem historiarum cognitionem.*

52. Agrippa D'Aubigné, *Histoire universelle*, ed. A. Thierry, 10 vols (Geneva, 1981-99).

53. ———, *Les Tragiques*, ed. J.-R. Fanlo (Paris, 2006).

54. Desiderius Erasmus, *'Copia': Foundations of the Abundant Style*, in *Collected Works*, xxiv, ed. C. Thompson, tr. and ed. B. Knott (Toronto, 1978).

55. Étienne de La Boétie, *Discours de la servitude volontaire*, ed. S. Goyard-Fabre (Paris, 1983).

56. Jean de La Taille, *Dramatic Works*, ed. K. Hall and C. Smith (London, 1972). In French.

57. *Traités de poétique et de rhétorique de la Renaissance*, ed. F. Goyet (Paris, 1990). Anthology of French treatises on poetics (Sebillet, Aneau, Peletier and Ronsard) and rhetoric (Fouquelin).

58. Marguerite de Valois, *Mémoires et autres écrits, 1574-1614*, ed. É. Viennot (Paris, 1999).

Studies

*Humanist poetry and poetics (see also **46-7**)*

59. G. Castor, *Pléiade Poetics* (Cambridge, 1964). On the theories that nourished the poetry of Ronsard and others.

60. T. Greene, *The Light in Troy: Imitation and Discovery in Renaissance*

Poetry (New Haven and London, 1982). On imitation as fraught, agonized. Includes chapters on Ronsard and Du Bellay.

Rhetoric

61. R. Lanham, *A Handlist of Rhetorical Terms* (Berkeley and Los Angeles, 1991). Useful for learning the system of rhetoric and the names of rhetorical figures.

Montaigne (see also *46*)

62. A. Tournon, *Montaigne en toutes lettres* (Paris, 1989).
63. T. Cave, *How to Read Montaigne* (London, 2007).

4

'My thoughts were elsewhere': Religion

We have considered how writers and thinkers imagined the times and places of ancient Greece and Rome. They also imagined a world that was not situated in time or space but transcended both: eternity. Often called the 'other world' ('l'autre monde'; **11**: p. 1533), it was divided between heaven and hell, God's kingdom and Satan's. For Catholics, the after-life also included purgatory, which, unlike heaven and hell, existed within time rather than beyond it. Although heaven and hell transcended space as well as time, they were commonly described in spatial terms, for want of any better language. On the other hand, the here-and-now on earth was unambiguously spatial, 'ce bas sejour', this 'low dwelling-place', which we are just passing through (**19**: p. 120).

Whereas detailed imagining of antiquity was done mainly by a social elite, this spiritual 'other world' was imagined by just about everyone, as it had been for centuries. However, its relationship to the here-and-now was bitterly contested – and no longer defined almost exclusively by the Roman Catholic Church – as religious divisions spread through Western Europe. Protestantism was born. This Reformation was one of the two greatest enduring schisms in the history of Christianity. (The other was the split from 1054 onwards between what then became the Eastern Orthodox and Western Roman Catholic churches.) The Huguenots (as French Protestants were known after 1560) did not succeed in displacing the Catholic Church in the way that happened in, say, England and much of Germany, but they numbered perhaps as many as two million by 1561 (roughly ten per cent of the population), not counting those who had fled France. Partly in response, there came a Catholic Counter-Reformation, which renewed Catholicism as well as combating Protestantism.

For educated Catholics and Protestants alike, the relationship between the mortal and the immortal world was not merely one between the here-and-now and a world beyond all space and time – the relationship was not bilateral, but trilateral. The third axis was history (antiquity, Middle Ages and so on), which had a (contested) relationship not only with the present – as we saw in the preceding chapters – but also with the eternal.

Earlier we saw Clément Marot – who wrote many worldly, courtly poems alongside religious ones – describing his thoughts as straying back and forth, even with a single poem, across the boundary between the mortal and immortal worlds: 'my thoughts were elsewhere'. Many readers nowadays, however they interpret heaven and hell, may feel reasonably familiar with the notion – whether or not they agree with it – that what we take in common parlance to be the 'real world' is in fact less real than an invisible, eternal world that subtends it. Indeed, that notion may be less unfamiliar now than the humanist one of reanimating antiquity. However, it is perhaps still difficult for us to appreciate just how pressing in sixteenth-century literature and thought was this sense of a spiritual vastness that awaits humans after death and yet also underlies everything they do in life.

4.1. Traditional Catholics and the 'other world'

Continuity between the here-and-now and eternity was emphasized by traditional Catholicism – Catholicism which was largely untouched by, or resistant to, the reforming ideas that spread in France especially from the fifteenth century and led to a schism from the 1530s. Traditional Catholicism sought to help believers bridge the gap between their present world and God's kingdom, where they could find salvation and eternal life. Here is a schematic account of this belief system (which glosses over many variations within it).

Going to heaven was only possible through God's merciful grace, which was freely given by Him, rather than earned by humans. But that distinction sometimes became blurred in practice, since people were able to put themselves in a position to receive grace, by partaking of the sacraments. There were seven of these: communion (the Eucharist), baptism, penance (confession), confirmation, extreme unction, marriage and ordination (of priests). Longing for grace was expressed through prayer, directed not only at God and Christ but at interceding figures such as the Virgin Mary and other saints.

Once one's sins were forgiven through God's grace, one still had to work off a 'temporal' penalty for them, a penance. The priest at confession stipulated its extent. Repentant sinners could then use their free will to choose to do good works that would earn merit in God's eyes and reduce the penalty owed. These might include helping the poor and sick, making a pilgrimage to pray at a saint's shrine, or building a road for the community. From the eleventh century, a practice had arisen where the Church formally granted whole or partial remission of someone's penalty if they had expressed contrition. The Church could grant such pardons, or indulgences, by drawing on a treasure store of surplus human merit, consisting of all the merit that Christ, the saints and other virtuous people had accumulated beyond what was necessary for their own salvation. This surplus could be distributed to repentant sinners who, to express gratitude, often gave money, for example as alms for the poor. But this had become difficult to distinguish from *buying* indulgences, which was not supposed to happen. Indulgences lessened the time someone was due to spend in purgatory. That was where souls went upon dying if they did not deserve to go straight to hell but still lacked sufficient merit to go straight to heaven. Time spent in purgatory could expiate one's remaining penalty.

Catholicism's broad assumption of a continuum between the natural and the supernatural was expressed by its trust in our five external senses. Material, 'sensible' objects (which can be touched, tasted and so on) could be a bridge between the two worlds. A striking example is bread and wine becoming Christ's body and blood in the Eucharist. But there were many others: paintings and sculptures of God, Christ, and the saints; candles for the dead; and relics, which were objects associated with Christ, a saint, or a holy event, and were venerated as earthly remnants of the divine.

While some of these beliefs and practices have survived into modern Western Catholicism, not all have. Some were attacked not only by Protestants but also by reforming Catholics. For example, Rabelais, an ex-Franciscan friar turned Benedictine monk, belonged to a strand of Catholicism now known as 'evangelism'. It was particularly prominent in some educated circles in France in the first half of the century. Influenced by Erasmus, it wanted reform but not schism. Like Protestants, evangelical Catholics attacked many of the practices that were believed by traditionalists to mediate between humans and God's kingdom. Evangelicals stressed that the main mediators should be Bible reading and prayer to Christ (not to the saints). They attacked the papacy, joining forces with Gallican Catholics. Without wishing to break with the Vatican, Gallicans such as the Cardinal Jean Du Bellay (whom Rabelais served in Rome) wanted the French Catholic Church to have greater independence from it. In the 'Gallican crisis' of 1550-52, because of political factors such as Pope Julius III's alliance with France's enemy the Habsburg Emperor Charles V, it even seemed possible that Henri II would follow the example of Anglicanism and England's Henry VIII in founding a national, non-Roman Catholic Church.

It was in this climate that Rabelais composed most of his *Fourth Book* (a few chapters were published in 1548, the full version in 1552). It snipes at Protestantism (in particular Calvinism) but reserves its most withering satire for the papacy. One of the islands that the friends visit during their voyage is inhabited by the 'Papimanes'. They worship not God but the Pope. Like God, he remains largely invisible, so the Papimanes are ready to venerate anyone who saw him. Their holy writ was the Decretals – Rabelais uses the term to refer to canon law decrees issued by popes from the twelfth century onwards. While Gallicans accepted the oldest of these, they resented later ones – some as recent as 1500 – as attempts by the Vatican to extend its worldly powers, for example by siphoning off more of the French Church's revenue.

The Papimane bishop, Homenaz, gives a mock encomium or eulogy of the Decretals. This epideictic set-piece ends with a peroration:

> Je disois doncques que ainsi vous adonnans à l'estude unicque des sacres Decretales, vous serez riches et honorez *en ce monde*. Je diz consequemment qu'*en l'aultre* vous serez infalliblement saulvez on benoist royaulme des Cieulx, du quel sont les clefz baillées à nostre bon Dieu Decretaliarche. O mon bon Dieu, lequel je adore, et ne veids oncques, de grace speciale ouvre nous en l'article de la mort, pour le moins, ce tressacré thesaur de nostre mere saincte Ecclise, du quel tu es protecteur, conservateur, promeconde, administrateur, dispensateur. Et donne ordre que ces precieux oeuvres de supererogation, ces beaulx pardons au besoing ne nous faillent. A ce que les Diables ne trouvent que mordre sus nos paouvres ames, que la gueule horrificque d'Enfer ne nous engloutisse. Si passer nous fault par Purgatoire, patience! en ton pouvoir et arbitre est nous en delivrer, quand vouldras. (**29**: p. 1147)

> So I was saying that, by devoting ourselves to the sole study of the holy Decretals, you will be rich and honoured *in this world*. I say consequently that *in the other* you will infallibly be saved in the blessed Kingdom of Heaven, the keys to which are given to our good Decretaliarch God. O my good God, Whom I adore and have never seen, by Thy special grace open unto us at the point of death, at least, that very sacred treasure of our mother holy church, of which Thou art the Protector, Preserver, Distributor, Adminstrator, Dispenser! [And give orders that those precious works of supererogation, those fine indulgences should not fail us in our need.] And see to it that the jaws of hell may not engulf us! If pass through purgatory we must, patience! In Thy power and will it lies to deliver us from it, if Thou wilt. (**30**: p. 554)

In reality, no pro-papal Catholic would have professed the view that the Decretals could save us in the 'other world' (let alone enrich us in this one). But Rabelais attributes that view to the Papimanes in order to present traditional Catholics as neglecting the Bible's power to transport us to that 'other world'. They resort instead to false mediation – indulgences. The Pope, who is the God addressed in Homenaz's prayer, dips into that store ('thesaur') of surplus merit that has been built up over the centuries through 'works of supererogation', that is, through good works done by Christ, the saints and others. The Pope redistributes some of that merit through indulgences ('pardons'). In this way he, not God, protects people from hell and decides how long they spend in purgatory.

This parody of Catholic prayer is so acerbic that it might strike readers new to Rabelais as blasphemous, anti-Catholic, even anti-religious. But the contexts of his life, times and works suggest otherwise. It is propaganda that implicitly promotes one Catholic view of our relation to eternity by exaggerating and ridiculing another Catholic view of it. Protestants also condemned indulgences. The 1517 attack on them by Martin Luther (1483-1546) is still seen by many as having inaugurated the Reformation. And the indulgence system was one of the many aspects of Catholicism to be reformed by the Council of Trent – the great Counter-Reformation meetings of the Church's leaders held in a city on the border of Italy and Austria between 1545 and 1563. The Council decreed that indulgences could be granted but not for money (not even alms). Pre-Tridentine (that is, pre-Trent) Catholicism has had – like scholasticism, to which it was intimately connected – a bad press in some scholarship on the French sixteenth century, although this is perhaps partly because vernacular attacks on it (by Rabelais, Clément Marot, Marguerite de Navarre and others) happen to have been more brilliant and so longer-lasting than defences of it. Only with the anti-Protestant poetry that Ronsard published from 1562 onwards did non-evangelical Catholicism gain a comparable vernacular champion in France.

4.2. Reformers and the 'other world'

In comparison with traditional Catholics, many reformers perhaps tended to emphasize more discontinuity between the here-and-now and the eternal world, at least in some respects. (By 'reformers' I mean Protestants and evangelical Catholics.) Yet even among reformers, the exact nature of the relation between the two worlds was contested.

4.2.1. Jean Calvin

The founding figure of French-speaking Protestantism was Jean Calvin. His theology was underpinned by a sense of the radical discontinuity between the human and the divine. A second-generation reformer, he followed Luther in drawing this sense of discontinuity from aspects of the thought of the early Church Father St Augustine. For all three thinkers, humans in their natural, fallen state are wholly flawed. Nothing in their nature prompts them to move towards the supernatural world. This contrasts with the scholasticism of much traditional Catholicism, derived from St Thomas Aquinas, who did consider that parts of human nature tend towards the supernatural. The Protestant view was also sharply opposed to, for example, the neo-Platonic theories of the soul's ascent which we encountered earlier and which posited a continuum from the human to the divine.

Calvin and Luther therefore rethought merit and grace, the twin concepts through which Catholics formulated their relation to the 'other world'. First, merit could not be earned through good works. Since for traditional Catholics accumulating merit led to remission of penalties that were due for sins, it was tantamount, the Protestants argued, to earning salvation. By contrast, they denied that humans could do anything whatsoever to increase their chances of entering heaven. They could only be saved ('justified') by faith, which meant entrusting their whole being to God. But humans could not decide to do that of their own volition. Only God could give them the gift of faith.

Secondly, to avoid any sense that we could actively dispose ourselves to receive grace, the dominant role of the sacraments was reduced by Calvin, Luther and Zurich's Huldrych Zwingli (1484-1531), who was the other major leader of the mainstream movements that have come to be known as the 'magisterial Reformation'. Calvin decreased the number of sacraments to the only two for which he could see a biblical foundation: baptism and communion. (Luther hesitated as to whether confession was a third sacrament.) Moreover, while these leaders still viewed the sacraments as God giving us grace, they played down the extent to which the sacraments bring us to the 'other world'. They also disagreed about this between themselves.

Take the example of the Eucharist. Catholics believe that its celebration at Mass brings the faithful into the real presence of Christ. When the priest repeats Christ's words 'This is my body', the bread and wine *become* Christ's body and blood through a process called transubstantiation. This concept was understood in terms of scholasticism's synthesis of Christianity with Aristotelianism. For Aristotle, the substance of an object, such as bread, is its essential bread-ness, what makes it bread as distinct from anything else. Its accidents are those aspects of it – taste, colour and shape – which can change without it having to become something other than bread. At the Eucharist, the bread and wine retain their sensible accidents, but their invisible substance changes into something divine. This was an opening up of the here-and-now to the invisible, immortal world.

For Calvin, on the other hand, the Eucharist brings us into the presence not of Christ's body, but of his body's spiritual substance. As Francis Higman has put it, the 'spiritual meaning [is] *conjoined* with the visible sign', but the sign – the bread and wine – does not itself physically change. There is still an opening up of the here-and-now to the invisible, immortal world, indeed more so than for Zwingli – for whom the spiritual event of the Eucharist consists only in its commemoration of Christ's past sacrifice – but for Calvin it is a more limited opening up than for Catholics and even Luther (despite Luther's rejection of transubstantiation), since for Catholics and Luther it involves, in different ways, Christ's body as well as his spirit (**65**: pp. 17-21). Calvin no longer sees the Eucharist as an irreplaceable mediator between the mortal and immortal worlds. For him, as for Zwingli, it is not indispensable to salvation: only faith is.

The Eucharistic bread and wine were just two of the many tangible objects which had long been believed by traditional Catholics to be gateways to the 'other world' and yet which Calvin, like other reformers, rethought or dispensed with. Others included paintings, sculptures, crucifixes, priestly vestments – and relics (against which Calvin wrote a dazzling 1543 treatise: **64**: pp. 183-249; **65**: pp. 47-97). He argued that the would-be transport to the 'other world' gets stuck at such objects, which become idolatrously worshipped in themselves and so are obstacles rather than mediators.

Whereas traditional Catholics filled the gulf between the human and the divine with practices (such as sacraments and good works) and objects that, if reverently attended to, gave them some hope of influencing their soul's destination, Calvin developed a doctrine of predestination which removed any hope of exerting this influence and so arguably widened the gulf. He drew this doctrine especially from St Augustine and Luther. Throughout and after the 1540s he gave it increasing weight, as did his followers after his death in 1564. Not all Protestants shared it. For example, Luther's follower Philipp Melanchthon (1497-1560) toned it down. According to Calvin, God has predestined everyone's soul once and for all to either salvation or damnation, and there is nothing we can do to change the decision.

However, although Calvin's theology widened in many respects the perceived gulf between the here-and-now and the 'other world', one could argue that in other respects it perhaps narrowed it. Calvin himself considered that Catholics placed between the two worlds not mediators but distractions, which actually distanced believers from God's kingdom rather than bringing them closer to it. He wrote in 1543:

> Car la Cène nous est donnée pour *nous faire élever nos esprits en haut au Ciel*, non pas pour les amuser à ces signes visibles du pain et du vin qui nous sont là présents. (**64**: p. 150)

> Because the gift of the Eucharist is intended to *raise our spirits up to heaven*, not to provide them with amusement through those visible signs of bread and wine which are present in it.

In Catholic hands, he argues, the bread and wine block rather than clear the path to heaven. Analogously, in a tract (probably 1556) against a Franciscan friar, Calvin presents Catholic teaching as over-emphasizing the need for a baby to be baptized with actual water in order for God's promised salvation of that baby's soul to be fulfilled. Catholics effectively damn the baby instead of realizing that he or she may go to heaven unbaptized:

> Vrai est que je dis bien, quand il plaira à Dieu de retirer *de ce monde* un enfant avant qu'on ait loisir de le baptiser, qu'il ne le faut pour tant tenir pour damné; et de cela j'allègue raisons et fondements, non pas tels que cet ivrogne babille, mais que la promesse de Dieu a bien assez de vertu pour les sauver. (**64**: p. 268)

> I do indeed say that when God chooses to withdraw a child *from this world* before it can be baptized, there is no reason to believe the child to be damned. Unlike that drunkard, I argue my case through sound reasoning and principles, which show that God's promise has sufficient power to save such children.

Besides, however wide Calvin believed the gulf between the human and divine worlds to be, he saw himself as helping to bridge it, notably by getting people to read and understand the Bible, 'la clef qui nous ouvre le Royaume de Dieu pour nous y introduire' ('the key which opens God's kingdom to let us in'; **64**: p. 50). This meant not only promoting and participating in a vernacular translation of it (first produced in 1535 by his relative Olivétan) but also devoting most of his voluminous writing to Bible commentaries. The Calvinist experience of sometimes reading Scripture for oneself and in French, rather than what had hitherto mainly been the Catholic one of only hearing it read aloud in Latin and then expounded by a priestly mediator, must have seemed more like a one-to-one with God. However, in practice, there was a new mediating authority – Calvin himself. Far from advocating a hermeneutic free-for-all, in his remarkable *Institution de la religion chrestienne* (*Institutes of the Christian Religion*) he claimed to demonstrate exactly what theology was contained in the Bible. The ever-expanding Latin versions of the *Institutes* that were published between 1536 and 1559 were each translated into French by Calvin himself and printed from 1541 to 1560. The *Institutes* gave readers the most detailed and sophisticated account of God's plans ever written in French, or indeed in any European vernacular, since Luther, brilliant user of German though he was, had not written systematic theology.

The project of bridging the gap between the here-and-now and the 'other world' was also lived out, spectacularly and experimentally, in the running of Geneva, the independent city-state that became Calvinism's centre. In the 1530s, many French supporters of reform left France to escape actual or likely repression. In 1533, Calvin himself went into hiding within France, in and beyond Paris, when suspected of having helped to write a distinctly evangelical, Lutheran-sounding sermon which his friend Nicolas Cop had preached soon after becoming rector of the University of Paris (whose theology faculty was the Sorbonne). Repression by various authorities – notably the Sorbonne, the Parlement of Paris and the monarchy, although not always in tandem – stiffened again after the so-called Affair of the Placards, when (on 18 October 1534) broadsheets denouncing the Catholic Mass were posted in Paris and elsewhere. The French émigrés initially went to a variety of cities, including Strasbourg and Basel. By the late 1540s, most were going to Geneva.

Calvin, who became sympathetic to reformist ideas at some point between 1529 and 1533, settled in 1536 – initially by semi-accident – in Geneva, which had recently accepted the Reformation. Calvin was persuaded to remain there by Guillaume Farel, in collaboration with whom he drafted a proposal for extending Church control over the populace. Each citizen was to sign a Confession of Faith. Refusal to sign would be punished by exile. Having failed to get the proposal implemented, and with the city council reasserting itself, Calvin and Farel were themselves banished in 1538. Calvin went to Strasbourg but was recalled in 1541 to Geneva, where he stayed until his death. He gave the Church a discipline unmatched by earlier reformers anywhere, and a new structure. It now included pastors (instead of priests) as well as other officers, and an ecclesiastical court (the Consistory) that policed citizens' morals, punishing anything from adultery to domestic violence, from dancing to gambling. Traditional Catholic practices, such as praying for the dead, were banned. Civic government was separate from the Church but, despite numerous political struggles, especially from 1555, the two worked together in trying to implement on earth Calvin's vision of a godly polity.

Surely, we might wonder, it was difficult for citizens to motivate themselves for this moral reorganization of daily life given the doctrine of predestination, according to which they could not influence their chances of reaching heaven? In practice, however, the doctrine seems to have had for many the paradoxical effect of making everyday life closer to God's kingdom. For, according to Calvin, although the composition of the invisible Church of the elect is known only by God, one sign that one belonged to it was virtuous behaviour. Another was adherence to the visible, earth-based Church, centred in Geneva. Moreover, from the rejection of the Catholic sacrament of priestly orders arose the Lutheran and Calvinist doctrine of the priesthood of all believers, according to which lay people were as close to God as were pastors (and could administer sacraments or preach). Calvin emphasized that each person had a special vocation or calling – as cobbler, weaver, pastor, woman or man – that had been decided by God's provi-

dence. This emphasis was doubtless very repressive in that it limited people's life options. But to many it may also have given a heightened sense of God's will being done on earth through them, as it is in heaven (to paraphrase the Lord's Prayer).

Many Calvinists also saw themselves as moving closer to heaven, even while on earth, by detaching themselves from a fundamental dimension of life on earth – place. Whereas many religions and belief-systems (such as modern-day nationalisms) are rooted in a sense of owning particular lands, Calvinism (unlike Lutheranism) was born in flight and exile. Although Calvin's hope was to convert France to the true Church, Protestants who lived where it was impossible for them to practise their religion were urged by him to go into exile if possible (**64**: pp. 127-81). For nobles whose families had owned the same land for centuries, this meant a huge renunciation not only of wealth but also of worldly identity:

> C'est une chose fâcheuse, que de se mettre en danger de perdre corps et biens, d'irriter tout le monde contre soi, d'être en oppropre et vitupère, de quitter le pays où on peut vivre à son aise, pour s'en aller en pays étrange comme à l'égarée. (**64**: p. 134)

> It's hard to risk losing your life and property, to make everyone angry with you, to be reviled and denounced, to leave one area, where you can live comfortably, for an unfamiliar one, as if you had got lost.

The refugee is thus doubly alienated, from the place left behind and from the one arrived at. But this helps him or her enter a spiritual place – that of the Church – that is not tied to human space, although its visible centre is Geneva. The elect can come closer to heaven while still on earth by accepting that earth, 'le monde' ('the world'), is in any case an alien place to them (**64**: p. 152).

So, although Calvin and Montaigne are about as different as two thinkers from the same period could be, they share a sense that what seems to be the present is in fact composed of otherness. Whereas

Montaigne is mainly concerned with the otherness that pervades our experience of the mortal world, Calvin is concerned to present that mortal world as a transitory shadow (**64**: p. 180), as being just as alien to the elect as were Egypt and Babylon to God's chosen people, the Israelites and Judaeans (**64**: p. 179).

This reveals the third side of the triangle: the present and the 'other world' relate not only to each other but also to human history. Although the triangle characterized all sixteenth-century religious thought, the nature of these relationships was contested. Calvinists aligned themselves with the subjugated Jews of the Old Testament. They drew comfort from those books of the Bible, such as the Psalms, which depicted righteous suffering at the hands of persecutors.

Like Protestants in general, Calvinists saw themselves as restoring a pure Church that had thrived in early Christianity before being overshadowed in the Middle Ages by Rome-led degradation. Calvinists denied the accusation that their Church was 'new'. If newness is fêted in much modern Western culture, it was often suspect in the sixteenth century, especially in religion. Rather, Calvinists saw themselves as peeling away layers of incorrect biblical exegesis plus extra-biblical doctrine and ritual that had accrued over centuries. They rejected the Catholic notion of history as a progressive tradition, in which God gradually supplements the Bible by revealing truths to Church fathers and Church councils. Although Calvin's Bible interpretations drew extensively on Church fathers (such as favourites St Augustine [354-430 CE] and St John Chrysostom [*c.* 347-407 CE]), he described himself as rejecting whatever was non-biblical even in their doctrine.

This Protestant view of history and of its relation to the present was nourished by humanism. Reformers applied the humanist return 'to the sources' (*ad fontes*) to biblical scholarship. Like Aristotle, the Bible had long been known in the West almost only in translation. The dominant version was the Vulgate, St Jerome's Latin translation from the fourth century CE. Humanists tried to establish and decode the original Hebrew of the Old Testament and the Greek of the New.

For example, Johannes Reuchlin, whom we encountered earlier, compiled a Hebrew manual (1506). In 1516, Erasmus published an edition of the New Testament in Greek along with a revised edition of the Latin Vulgate. A leading figure in early French humanism, the Aristotelian and evangelical Catholic Jacques Lefèvre d'Étaples, published in 1512 a commentary on St Paul's epistles that was informed by the original Greek (although his Greek was limited in comparison with Budé's), as was his later French translation of the New Testament (1523). Such ventures had an unsettling effect on traditional Catholic doctrine. For example, Lefèvre d'Étaples's commentary on St Paul stressed that humans could only be saved by faith, not by works. He argued this even before Luther.

So, by the time Calvin based his biblical exegesis on Hebrew and Greek versions, he was following in the footsteps of both Catholic and Protestant humanists. Indeed, until a schism became entrenched in the French-speaking world, reformers were not clearly divided between 'Protestant' and 'Catholic'. Whereas the biblical scholarship of Erasmus had been conducted more in a relatively open-minded spirit than for confessional point-scoring, from about the 1530s there was a greater tendency for French Catholic and Protestant theologians alike to use humanism to shore up their own Church, and to play down those aspects of antiquity which they found threatening. If many Catholics were worried by the Greek or Hebrew terms lying behind time-consecrated Latin doctrinal concepts, many Calvinists were worried by the syncretist embracing of 'pagan' myth and culture.

4.2.2. Théodore de Bèze, 'Abraham sacrifiant'

Calvinist variations on the triangular relationship between the here-and-now, the past and eternity, were played out not only in theological tracts but in numerous other kinds of writing. For example, in 1550 a play called *Abraham sacrifiant* (*Abraham's sacrifice*) was performed by students of the Lausanne Academy on their graduation day, probably in the city's cathedral. It was by Théodore de

Bèze, who was then Professor of Greek at the Academy and later succeeded Calvin as leader of the Genevan Church.

In the biblical episode (Genesis 22) that the play recounts, God tests Abraham by ordering him to kill sacrificially his only son, Isaac. The anguished Abraham agrees. Just as his knife is about to fall, an angel intervenes to stop him. He has passed the test.

Why did Bèze choose this subject? For Protestants in general, Abraham epitomized total faith in God. The incomprehensible, apparently brutal nature of God's command only serves in the play to highlight, on the one hand, the enormous gulf that separates our world from God's, our understanding from His. Bèze emphasized the pain of that gulf by labelling the play a 'tragedy' on the title page of the printed version. The label looked new. Indeed, it had never been given to a French-language play before.

Yet, on the other hand, that gulf is bridged by faith, by Abraham's extraordinary trust and obedience. The play also hammers home that point, which perhaps explains why Bèze observes in the preface that the play is in fact part comedy, not in the sense of being funny but in certain technical respects and, presumably, because it has a happy ending. Indeed, with French-language imitations of Greco-Roman drama taking off in the years immediately following Bèze's play, contemporaries were sensitive to the relation between plot and genre. La Taille, in his 1572 preface on the art of tragedy, argued that Bèze was wrong to call a play with a happy ending a tragedy (**56**: p. 20). This controversial generic ambiguity stems from the two ways of interpreting the play. Does it represent the here-and-now and the 'other world' as being close to each other or far apart?

Theatre, which puts real bodies in physical spaces, also enabled Bèze to enact on various levels that tragedy of *place* that was central to the Calvinist diaspora's experience of the relation between the human and divine worlds. An actor recites the prologue. Bèze encourages him to gesture towards his surroundings – the set, which was probably a wooden structure or painted canvas – with the words 'Maintenant donc icy est le païs / Des Philistins' ('Here then is the

country of the Philistines'; ll. 25-6). Abraham's first words present it
as an alien place: 'Depuis que j'ay mon païs delaissé, / Et de courir
çà et là n'ay cessé' ('Since abandoning my country and running this
way and that [...]'; ll. 49-50). 'Although I am 74' (continues
Abraham), 'You have ordered me to leave my homeland': 'Or donc
sortir tu me fis de ces lieux, / Laisser mes biens, mes parens, et leurs
dieux' ('So you made me leave that place, abandoning my property,
my family, and their gods'; ll. 71-2). Bèze thus gives enormous
prominence to the fact that in Genesis (22:2-4) God commanded
Abraham to make the sacrifice after a three-day journey from home.
And Bèze adds the detail about fleeing a country of false gods. The
words just quoted could have been spoken by countless Calvinist
refugees. Indeed, Bèze echoes them in his voice at the start of the
preface: 'Il y a environ deux ans, que Dieu m'a faict la grace d'ha-
bandonner le païs auquel il est persecuté, pour le servir selon sa
saincte volonté' ('About two years ago, God gave me grace to
abandon the country where he is persecuted and serve him
according to his holy will'; p. 45). In 1548, the 29-year-old Bèze had
forsaken family, fortune and friends in France to go to Geneva.

Another specificity of theatre is its capacity to make present
bodies act out the deeds of dead ones. Bèze exploits this in order to
connect the here-and-now to history. The preface states that
Abraham is one of the greatest three of a 'multitude d'exemples' (p.
45) from sacred history who have had a real, living influence on
Bèze's own behaviour. This is the religious version of the system of
exemplarity. Drama, perhaps more than other genres, can capture
the dead's active impact on the living by symbolically embodying
the dead in actors. Bèze makes playfully explicit the superimposi-
tion of past times and places on present ones. Here again is the actor
reciting the prologue:

> Tu penses estre au lieu ou tu n'es pas.
> Plus n'est icy Lausanne, elle est bien loin:
> Mais toutesfois quand il sera besoin,
> Chacun pourra, voire dedans une heure,

Sans nul danger retrouver sa demeure.
Maintenant donc icy est le païs
Des Philistins. Estes vous esbaïs? (ll. 20-6)

You think you are in a place where you are not. This is no longer
Lausanne – it's far away. But you'll all be able to return home safely
when necessary, in only an hour's time. Here then is the country of
the Philistines. Are you astonished?

The principle of such time-and-place travel was familiar from
mystery and miracle plays, which staged stories from the Bible or
from saints' lives. But Bèze is stressing that thanks to his short new
genre, such imaginary travel does not have to take days on end, as
did mystery plays, which were now on the wane.

Although various aspects of this new genre, including its relative
brevity, imitate ancient drama, Bèze is trying *not* to evoke the
Greco-Roman ancient world. He explains in the preface that in the
canticle sections (loosely modelled on the ancient Greek chorus) he
has avoided Greek terms such as 'strophes' and 'antistrophes',
which would 'espoventer les simples gens' ('terrify uneducated
people'; pp. 49-50). Despite its origins in the Lausanne Academy,
the play explicitly addresses the less educated too (ll. 1-2). By mainly
using the low rhetorical register (*genus humile*) and writing the decasyllabic and octosyllabic lines in ways that evoke (without actually
reproducing) everyday language, Bèze is not only, like many
Calvinist writers, reacting against Pléiade-style elitist humanism. He
is also making it easier for the audience to imagine that they really
are spending an hour in an Old Testament land, since the people
there talk a bit like them.

4.2.3. The Wars of Religion and Agrippa D'Aubigné's 'Les Tragiques'

The more difficult was life in the here-and-now, the further it could
seem from the spiritual 'other world' and the more that distance
could seem tragic. So, when in 1616 the Huguenot D'Aubigné first

published an enormous poem (then 8,502 lines long), that he had begun in 1577 and would continue revising till his death in 1630, he called it *Les Tragiques*, because it recounted the suffering of true believers at the hands of Catholics over the centuries, and in particular during the recent Wars of Religion.

The intermittent civil wars dominated life in France from 1562 to 1598, with religion just one of their many causes. Another was factionalism among France's great noble families. After the death of Henri II in 1559, three of his sons became the next kings (François II, Charles IX and Henri III) until 1589. Their mother Catherine de' Medici was periodically in control of government, given the initial youth of the first two kings. Whereas, as we saw earlier, the reigns of François Ier and Henri II saw the monarchy's power increase on the whole, these subsequent reigns saw it decrease, sometimes drastically. From 1559, the efforts of three factions in particular to counter-balance, control or even replace the Valois monarchy intensified: the Guises, the Bourbons and the Montmorencys. Many Guises were Catholics of a kind unwilling to tolerate any Protestantism. On the other hand, some members of the Bourbons (the prince of Condé) and the Montmorencys (Admiral Coligny) became Huguenots. In 1560, the Guises were in the ascendant: François II's wife Mary Stuart (Queen of Scots) was from their family. That year they foiled a plot, possibly involving Condé, to kidnap Mary's boy-king husband and put him under Protestant influence (the 'Conspiracy of Amboise').

Religion made these factional politics more explosive. In 1559, the Calvinist Church in France held its first National Synod, having become less clandestine. In 1561 Catherine de' Medici tried to offset a descent into violence by organizing the Colloquy of Poissy, aimed at achieving some religious conciliation between Catholics and Protestants. (Bèze led the Protestant delegation.) But in March 1562 a massacre of Protestants by the duke of Guise at Vassy sparked the first civil war.

There were many more atrocities, the worst being the St Bartholomew's Day massacres of 1572. By then, the Guises had lost their ascendancy. The marriage took place between the young Bourbon and Huguenot prince, Henri de Navarre, and Charles IX's sister, Marguerite de Valois (whose memoirs we encountered earlier). The idea was to reconcile Huguenots to the monarchy. The Huguenot nobility gathered in Paris for the event, but an initially unsuccessful attempt to assassinate Coligny led to a spiral of violence in which about 10,000 Huguenots were murdered by Catholics in Paris and elsewhere. Later in 1572, Calvinist fortress towns such as La Rochelle and Sancerre came under royal-led siege. (The Calvinist pastor Jean de Léry wrote a harrowing account of life inside besieged Sancerre.)

By 1576, the Protestant position had strengthened once more and the latest in a series of truces was signed. Probably because Henri III had signed this 'Peace of Monsieur' from a position of weakness, it gave Protestants even greater freedom of worship than previous edicts (of 1562 and 1563). This enraged those Catholics, led by the Guises, who wished to simply eradicate the new heresy. So in 1576 they formed a Catholic League (*Ligue*), followed by another in 1584 when, to their alarm, the Huguenot Henri de Navarre became heir to the throne. The Leaguers (*ligueurs*) were openly hostile to Henri III. Thus, much of the conflict was now Catholic against Catholic. Philip II of Spain entered the fray to support the League in 1584. In 1588, Henri III fled from pro-League Paris but then had the two leading Guises murdered. He himself was assassinated in 1589, and so Henri de Navarre became a contested Henri IV. France only had a Protestant king until 1593, when he converted to Catholicism. This enabled him to bring Paris back under royal control in 1594.

The party now in the ascendant was that of the *Politiques* – moderate Catholics and Protestants who desired peace and freedom from foreign interference more than they desired the eradication of the opposing religion. Although the term *Politiques* only came into common use in 1584 the attitude went back to the Chancellor Michel de l'Hospital in the 1560s and is adumbrated in the 1561 *Memoire sur la pacification des troubles* (*How to End the Unrest*) attributed to Montaigne's friend La Boétie. In 1594, some *Politiques* got their influential, anti-League *Satyre Ménippée* (*Menippean Satire*) into print, but only by 1598 were the League and its Spanish allies defeated. That year, the Edict of Nantes became the latest to grant limited freedom of worship to Protestants. Although it lasted until 1685 (when it was revoked), discontent continued on all sides.

Discontent certainly continued for the Huguenot D'Aubigné. According to his *Tragiques*, the history of the true Church in France has not had a happy ending, but will eventually. Henri IV, D'Aubigné's erstwhile friend, turned traitor. But only in the here-and-now was the true religion defeated. In the 'other world', its persecutors would be punished, and the elect rewarded. *Les Tragiques* is structured by this disjunction between the mortal and immortal worlds. The 'tragedy' is traumatic. It is dominant in the lives of the faithful and in most of the poem. But, in the perspective of eternity, it turns out to have been only temporary.

Of the seven books, the first five focus on the recent French past, while also aligning its persecuted victims with their biblical and other forebears. Books 1-3 outline respectively the pitiful state of France, its Catholic rulers' decadence and the legal system's corruption ('Misères', 'Princes', 'La chambre dorée'). Books 4-5 are, if anything, bleaker still. They concern: first, the Protestants and earlier dissenters who were individually executed for heresy by the judicial system and so qualify as martyrs ('Les feux'; **69**: pp. 40-5); then, the more general mass of Protestants who were persecuted in recent times ('Les fers'). Only in Books 6-7 does the resolution of tragedy predominate, first *within* human history, as D'Aubigné lists the punishments that have befallen persecutors while they were alive ('Vengeances'), and then *outside* human history, when he describes the Apocalypse at which time stops and everyone is consigned to heaven or hell ('Jugement'). For D'Aubigné this is not a remote prospect. He predicts it will happen in the year 1666 (v, l. 1416) – he shares many of his contemporaries' taste for Bible-based calculations of the world's life span.

Although the mortal world is foregrounded most, there are continuous reminders of the immortal world from which it is tragically separated. The relation between the two is one of inversion. Since the here-and-now is 'inside-out' (a 'mond' à l'envers', i, l. 235), success within it is often actually a sign of failure in the 'other world'. This is the message of consolation, reassurance and hope that D'Aubigné offers his co-religionaries. He sometimes superimposes the immortal world on the mortal one by distinguishing between the earthly events narrated and the heavenly viewpoint from which they are narrated. Thus, in 'Les fers', events in the Wars of Religion from the St Bartholomew's Day massacres onwards are recounted in the form of a prophetic dream which, the poet claims, was granted to him as he lay critically wounded in the aftermath of those massacres (v, ll. 1195-). D'Aubigné is here alluding to the moment at which he started writing *Les Tragiques.* To maximize that moment's significance, he rearranges what had actually happened: he was indeed badly wounded in 1572 (at Talcy), but not necessarily for religious reasons, whereas it was only later, in 1577 – when wounded again (at Casteljaloux), this time while fighting for the reformers – that he seems to have begun writing *Les Tragiques.*

The poet claims that this dream or fainting fit transported his spirit to where it spent seven hours viewing celestial paintings that angels had made of past and future episodes of the Wars of Religion (v, ll. 261-). Despite the rejection of neo-Platonism by much Calvinism, this round trip to the 'other world' owes something to that philosophy. The rhetorical technique of *ekphrasis* – verbal description of a non-verbal artefact such as a painting or sculpture – enables the poet to emphasize, even while recounting atrocities, that all will end well. It also stresses that all martyrdoms will be *remembered* (v, l. 1265). Like the poem itself, the paintings are memorials. With the allegiance of many French Calvinists to the monarchy decreasing during the Wars of Religion, martyrology thrived (most famously with Jean Crespin's *Livre des martyrs*, 1554-70), telling them that they belonged to a spiritual community rather than to the earthly kingdom of France that they had previously mistaken for an image of God's kingdom.

If *Les Tragiques* often emphasizes the gulf between the here-and-now and the 'other world', it also makes poetry a way of narrowing the gulf. The celestial paintings are one example. Another is the vision of the future resurrection of the dead (in 'Jugement'):

> C'est faict, Dieu vient reigner, de toute prophetie
> Se void la periode à ce poinct accomplie.
> La terre ouvre son sein, du ventre des tombeaux   665
> Naissent des enterrez les visages nouveaux:
> Du pré, du bois, du champ, presque de toutes places,
> Sortent les corps nouveaux, et les nouvelles faces:
> Icy les fondements des chasteaux rehaussez
> Par les ressuscitans promptement sont percez: 670
> Icy un arbre sent des bras de sa racine
> Grouiller un chef vivant, sortir une poictrine:
> Là l'eau trouble bouillonne, et puis s'esparpillant
> Sent en soy des cheveux, et un chef s'esveillant:
> Comme un nageur venant du profond de son plonge: 675
> Tous sortent de la mort, comme l'on sort d'un songe.
> Les corps par les tyrans autrefois deschirez
> Se sont en un moment en leurs corps asserrez:
> Bien qu'un bras ait vogué par la mer escumeuse
> De l'Affricque bruslee en Tyle froiduleuse,   680
> Les cendres des bruslez volent de toutes parts,
> Les brins plustot unis qu'ils ne furent esparts
> Viennent à leur posteau, en cette heureuse place
> Riants au ciel riant, d'une aggreable audace.

It's all over: God comes to reign. At this moment, all prophecies are fulfilled. The Earth's breast opens; from the belly-like graves are born the new faces of people who were buried in the earth. From meadows, woods, fields and virtually every spot there emerge new bodies, new faces. Here, castles are lifted into the air as resurrected people spontaneously poke up through their foundations. Here, a tree can feel a living head and a human chest emerging from the arm of its root. There, the choppy water, boiling over, feels within itself splayed hair and a waking head. Like a swimmer surfacing from a deep dive, they all emerge from death as one emerges from a dream. Bodies previously torn apart by tyrants have now been instantaneously remoulded into bodies. Although an arm crossed the foamy ocean from burnt Africa to frozen Thule, the ashes of those who were burned now fly back together from all directions, and the various bits – reunited more quickly than they were separated – return to the executioner's stake, that happy place, where with due boldness they smile at the smiling heavens.

As Frank Lestringant has pointed out, D'Aubigné's *elocutio*, his way of writing about this future fulfilment of the Old Testament prophecies (ll. 663-4) turns that future into a present, a here-and-now. The 'now' is emphasized by the present tense that D'Aubigné uses instead of the future tense we might have expected; the 'here' is emphasized by the deictic terms 'Icy' and 'Là' (ll. 669, 671, 673; **4**: pp. 465-5). ('Deixis' means pointing to a precise context.)

The reassembling of bodies is not 'just' a poetic image. D'Aubigné follows Calvin in arguing that it will happen literally. Although in many ways Calvinism tried to separate body from spirit in reaction to the material culture of Catholicism, on the other hand the doctrine of the bodily resurrection of the dead projects the physical body onto eternity. By focusing with such shocking precision on the voyages of individual body parts and remnants (ashes), D'Aubigné conveys the awe of this moment at which human history crashes into eternity. In terms of the *dispositio* of *Les Tragiques*, the reassembling of bodies acts as a counterpoint to the more distressing, but less strange *dis*integration of martyrs' bodies that has been much described in the poem's preceding books. D'Aubigné's narratives of burnings at the stake are now replayed in reverse (ll. 682-4).

The passage tells us that 'reality', the here-and-now, is not what it seems. It will one day be reversed. Bodies will burst out of apparently fixed objects – trees, castles. The subtexts here include Ovid's *Metamorphoses* – in which people or deities turn into animals or plants – and numerous sixteenth-century works, from Ronsard to Montaigne, which emphasize the world's mutability. But through imitation of Ovid, the Bible (for example the image of God enthroned on Judgement Day, 1. 663), and many other texts, D'Aubigné has created poetry unlike any other. The metamorphosis and movement he describes is incorporated into the writing itself – his version of sixteenth-century abundant style (*copia*), with his verbal extravagance, his neologisms, his lists of near-synonyms, his high quotient of terms denoting the physical world, his thick texture of rhetorical figures and his heavy repetition and word play (all of which soon became unfashionable with a new vogue for pared-down, 'neo-classical' language).

For example, the meaning of 'bras' in line 671 slips from a tree-root's wooden arm to a human's fleshly arm, which 'bras' then denotes more clearly in line 679. The repetition 'bruslee'/'bruslez' merges the burnt ashes of martyrs with the burnt Africa to which they once blew (ll. 680-1). The repetition of 'Riants'/'riant' within a single hemistich merges the martyrs' smile with Heaven's. One of D'Aubigné's favourite rhetorical figures, *polyptoton* – repeating different words which share the same root – constantly erodes boundaries between distinct objects, as when 'des enterrez' emerge from 'La terre' (ll. 665-6). The water in which the corpses awake becomes that out of which the diver reappears: because water is common to both terms of this comparison, they partly merge with each other – simile turns into metonymy (ll. 675-6). (Simile is a comparison based on a word such as 'like'. Metonymy designates one thing by naming something else to which it is somehow closely connected in reality.)

As we saw earlier with Ronsard (whose poetry D'Aubigné admired, despite their religious differences), verbs are crucial to poetry that seeks to incorporate such mobility, especially verbs which themselves denote change or movement (*sortir*, which occurs four times here, *naître* and so on). D'Aubigné makes verbs prominent by positioning them at the start of lines (ll. 668, 672, 674, 683) and at the start (l. 672) or the middle (l. 676) or the end (l. 673) of successive hemistichs. The depth of the earth's sudden opening is evoked by the length and openness of the first vowel sound of 'ouvre' (l. 665); the vowel is elongated because followed by a sounded neutral 'e'. '[O]uvre' also stands out because it follows another stressed word ('terre'), producing an awkward, unusual '2:1:3' in this line's first hemistich, as if the earth is heaving with the strain. Elsewhere too, D'Aubigné uses open vowels to suggest the depth of the abyss which is now opening up: note the assonance in 'du profond de son plonge: / [...] songe' (ll. 675-6) – just one example of the passage's dense musical texture, reliant less on rich end-rhymes than on sustained assonance and alliteration.

D'Aubigné is trying to make the ecstatic transition to the 'other world' gripping, rather than boring, as it might have been had he relied, say, only on the figure of antithesis (ll. 681-2) which is fundamental to all Calvinist writing (including his own) about the relationship between heaven and earth. If the ecstasy is gripping, that is perhaps because even this imagined present is not absolute. It is not devoid of otherness and absence, since ecstasy is still described in terms of desire rather than of ultimate fulfilment, in terms of movement towards a destination rather than arrival at it. Hence the forwards-movement of bodies created in line 667 by the gradated pattern of clauses (2:2:2|6). Hence too, in the following line (668), the chiasmus (ABBA pattern) and *polyptoton* which inject movement into the potentially repetitive and static notion of 'novelty'.

Even as D'Aubigné describes the eternal end of the human story, the desire *for* that end is the most prominent. If he uses the celestial paintings of 'Les fers' to imagine viewing earth from heaven, in 'Jugement' it is always emphasized that heaven (like hell) is being viewed from earth. Since heaven is a 'place' that cannot be adequately represented by human language (v, ll. 18-20), paradoxically its representation becomes perhaps slightly less inadequate when language points to something beyond itself and announces, after thousands of lines, its own imminent silencing. Here are the poem's last words:

> Le coeur ravy se taist, ma bouche est sans parolle:
> Tout meurt, l'ame s'enfuit, et reprenant son *lieu*
> Extaticque se pasme au giron de son Dieu. (vii, ll. 1217-18)

> The heart, transported, falls silent; my mouth is wordless; everything
> dies; the soul flies off and, swooning ecstatically, returns to its place
> in the lap of its God.

4.2.4. Marguerite de Navarre, 'L'Heptaméron'

Calvinists were not alone in emphasizing the discontinuity between the here-and-now and the 'other world'. Some Catholic evangelicals did so too, including the woman who became their fulcrum and protector.

Marguerite d'Angoulême became Marguerite d'Alençon on her first marriage in 1509, and Marguerite de Navarre on her second in 1527. Her younger brother became king, as François Ier, in 1515. Having probably shared his tutors, she was educated to an unusual degree even for an aristocratic woman. In the early years of her brother's reign, she periodically acted as diplomat and informal political counsellor. She also became immersed in evangelical thinking: she knew Lefèvre d'Étaples from 1518 and corresponded from 1521 to 1524 with Guillaume Briçonnet, a bishop who had enlisted Lefèvre d'Étaples in his attempt to reform the Catholic Church by starting with his own diocese of Meaux. By the early 1530s, Marguerite de Navarre was strongly resented by the Sorbonne as a promoter of what it saw as heresy. Probably in the early 1520s, she had begun writing extraordinary devotional works, sometimes exploring mysticism as well as evangelism. They eventually included poems, plays and verse-dialogues. In 1533, the Sorbonne initially condemned the second edition of her *Miroir de l'âme pécheresse* (*Mirror of a Sinful Soul*), before backtracking under pressure from her brother the King. After the 1534 Affair of the Placards, she could no longer rely on his cooperation in her support for evangelical reform, and her court in French Navarre, in the South West, became a periodic haven for evangelicals such as Clément Marot (1534-35), who had long been in her service, and Lefèvre d'Étaples, who died there in 1536.

In about 1542, she started composing stories based on recent events she had heard about or witnessed in the lives of all ranks of people, from the King down to a boat-woman (*L'Heptaméron*, Novellas 25 and 5). Imitating Giovanni Boccaccio's fourteenth-century *Decameron* – of which she commissioned a 1545 French translation – she developed a frame narrative in which ten fictional interlocutors tell each other ten stories per day, for ten days. She only completed just over seven days before her death in 1549 – hence the title *L'Heptaméron* that was given to the collection in its first more or less complete (if inaccurate) edition, in 1559.

Compared with her more emphatically other-worldly writings, at first glance *L'Heptaméron* seems this-worldly. It tells of sex, violence, power, deceit, corruption and money. In deliberate contrast to the genre of romance (*le roman*) – such as the popular *Amadis de Gaule*, which set overtly fictitious adventures in a mythic, remote past – the *Heptaméron* situates events mostly in France and in recent times. Although names are changed or withheld, some of the stories' protagonists can be traced back to real historical figures, including Marguerite de Navarre herself. And the interlocutors agree only to recount events that actually happened (p. 65).

However, these are not conventional novellas. They agonize constantly over the relation between this 'real' world of recent events and the 'other world' of eternity. Boccaccio had done nothing of the kind. Marguerite de Navarre builds up her frame narrative far beyond his. Her interlocutors discuss the behaviour of each novella's protagonists from a range of perspectives, from the other-worldly – including at times the neo-Platonic (pp. 242-4) – to the this-worldly. Another departure from Boccaccio is that the ten interlocutors are split evenly between the sexes, whereas

Boccaccio's women outnumbered the men by seven to three. Although some female voices (such as Parlamente and Oisille) are represented as more authoritative than some male ones (such as Hircan), none emerges as conclusive. For Marguerite de Navarre, in contrast with D'Aubigné, the relation between the mortal and immortal worlds is *so* disjunctive that human attempts to pin it down are just shots in the dark.

The question is not just how to get from here to heaven when we die, but how to live in this world given that it is so fallen. Oisille's evangelical answer is that we should not have absolute faith in anyone in this world, even an apparently loyal lover or (in the story she is about to recount) an apparently holy friar. Such mediators, always potentially fallible, can mislead us,

> de sorte que vostre foy divertie de ce droict chemin, s'estime trouver salut en quelque autre creature, qu'en celuy seul qui ne veult avoir compaignon à nostre creation et redemption, lequel est tout puissant pour nous sauver *en la vie eternelle, et en ceste temporelle* nous consoler et delivrer de toutes noz tribulations […] (p. 286)

> [so] that your faith, diverted from the straight and narrow path, seeks salvation in some other creature rather than in Him alone who desired no companion in our creation and redemption, in Him alone who is almighty to save us *unto eternal life and in this temporal life* to console us and deliver us from all our tribulations […] (**67**: p. 266)

For Oisille, we can open ourselves to this eternal salvation and temporal consolation by loosening our attachments to the here-and-now. Indeed, the frame narrative imagines precisely such a loosening. In the Prologue, the ten aristocratic interlocutors take refuge in an abbey – Nostre Dame de Serrance (p. 61) – as survivors of a flood (in Boccaccio it was a plague). They can only return to their various homes once a bridge has been built. This will take at least ten days (p. 62). Oisille suggests they use this detachment from their usual places, this dis-location, as an opportunity. If (she says) you devote each day, as she normally does anyway, to prayer, Bible-reading and (on a non-Protestant note) the Mass, then 'vous trouverrez en ce desert la beauté qui peult estre en toutes les villes' ('you will find even in this wilderness all the beauty a city could afford'; p. 64; **67:** p. 67). The material 'desert' – a place devoid of customary diversions – will become a spiritual one, in which the absence of self-centred concerns makes God's love more powerfully felt. But Hircan is not persuaded:

> Ma dame ceux qui ont leu la saincte Escriture (comme je croy que nous tous avons faict) confesseront vostre dire estre veritable: mais si fault il que vous regardiez, que nous ne sommes encore si mortifiez qu'il ne nous faille quelque passetemps et exercice corporel. Car si nous sommes en noz maisons, nous avons la chasse et la vollerie, qui nous faict passer, et oublier mille folles pensées [...] (p. 64)

> Madame, anyone who has read the holy Scriptures – as indeed I think we all have here – will readily agree that what you have said is true. However, you must bear in mind that we have not yet become so mortified in the flesh that we are not in need of some sort of amusement and physical exercise in order to pass the time. After all, when we're at home, we've got our hunting and hawking to distract us from the thousand and one foolish thoughts that pass through one's mind [...] (**67:** p. 67)

Hircan ironically concedes that he and the others have not gone far down the path to mortification which, for monks and mystics, was the process of dying to this world in order to be alive to the 'other world'. In contrast with this *process* or journey, everyday pleasures are pure repetition: spiritually empty, they do nothing but pass the time. We might as well spend our life staring at a clock.

This exchange between Oisille and Hircan sets up a this- versus other-worldly tension that persists throughout the frame narrative. The daily timetable that the interlocutors adopt is a compromise between the claims of the two worlds. After getting up, the interlocutors hear Oisille read from and gloss the Bible, before they hear Mass. But then, after a ten-o'clock breakfast, they take turns telling stories from midday to four o'clock. Next they return to prayer, joining the abbey's monks for Vespers. Finally, they have supper, play games and retire to bed (pp. 66-7, 160).

For most readers, then and now, the most immediately attractive and accessible parts of the *Heptaméron* are perhaps the stories themselves, with the interlocutor's discussions of them coming second, and the descriptions of the devotional routine that are given at the start and end of each day coming third. But, like the interlocutors, we are challenged to reassess our priorities. Halfway through the projected ten days, at the end of the fifth, Oisille worries that the stock of amazing stories will run out. Geburon disagrees:

> Guebron leur dist, que tant que *le monde* dureroit, se feroient tous le[s] jours cas dignes de memoire : 'car la malice des hommes mauvais, est tousjours telle qu'elle a esté, comme la bonté des bons: et tant que la malice et bonté regneront *sur la terre*, il[s] la rempliront tousjours de nouveaux actes: combien qu'il soit escrit, qu'il ne se faict "rien nouveau sous le soleil". Mais nous, qui n'avons esté appellez au conseil privé de Dieu, ignorans les premieres causes, trouvons toutes choses nouvelles, et tant plus admirables, que moins nous les vouldrions, ou pourrions faire. Parquoy n'ayez peur que les journées, qui viendront, ne suivent bien celles qui sont passées [...]' (p. 467)

> However, Geburon assured her that as long as *the world* endured there would be plenty of things worth recounting. 'For the wickedness of evil men is the same now as it always has been. So too is the goodness of good men. As long as good and evil reign *on the earth*, the earth will be filled with new deeds, even though it is written that there is nothing new under the sun. For we, who have not been called to God's privy council and who are ignorant of the first causes of things, find all things new, and the less we are able or willing to do them ourselves, the more wonderful we find them. Therefore have no fear that the days that are left will not be as good as those that have passed [...]' (**67**: p. 427)

The stories entertain because they *seem* endlessly diverse. They are novelties, *nouvelles*, in the sense that they have not even been written down before, it is claimed (p. 559). But, the other-worldly perspective provided by the Bible (Ecclesiastes 1:10) reveals that they are in fact – like the daily pleasures described above by Hircan – pure repetition, since there is nothing new under the sun. By contrast, the parts of *L'Heptaméron* that seem at first glance to be pure repetition – the starts and ends of days – turn out on closer inspection to describe a progression. Initially, the interlocutors are keener on the stories than on their prayers, for which they are chronically late. But they become more punctual and enthusiastic as the days pass, losing a sense of 'real' time as their thoughts turn more to eternity (p. 522).

By the same token, although the sequence of the 72 stories does not follow any neat overall pattern (and varies between manuscripts), it is striking that the theme of mortification, of dying to this world, that is implicit in so many, becomes particularly prominent in some later ones, such as Novellas 64 (p. 541) and 67. Novella 67 is a partly fictionalized account of an episode that really did occur on the 1542-43 voyage to Canada by Roberval (Chapter 7 below). In the *Heptaméron* version, Roberval abandons on an uninhabited island two of his party, a married couple, since the husband had betrayed Roberval. The couple's absolute dependence on God (p. 550) is actualized in a literal way by their helplessness in this strange land ('terre estrange', p. 549). Indeed, this drama of dis-location is a more austere version of the Prologue's flood. The wife reads the Bible incessantly, with an exclusive evangelical-style focus on the New Testament (p. 550). She spends her days in the way that Oisille would have liked the interlocutors to. The key term from the Prologue returns twice, once as the husband dies: 'il passa joyeusement de ce *desert* en la celeste patrie' ('he passed joyously from this [wilderness] into the regions of Heaven'; p. 551; **67**: p. 504). The wife does not die, except in the sense of mortification, which paradoxically liberates her spirit to live more fully:

Ainsi vivant, quant au corps de vie bestiale, et quant à l'esprit de vie angelique, passoit son temps en lectures, contemplations, prieres et oraisons, ayant un esprit joyeux, et contant dedans un corps amaigry et demy mort. (p. 551)

And so she lived on, her bodily existence no higher than that of the beasts, but her soul in the sphere of the angels. For she spent her time in reading the Scriptures, in contemplation, prayer and other devotions. Her soul, within her emaciated and half-dead body, was joyous and contented. (**67**: p. 504)

At this point, the narrative has ground to a halt. The story it recounts (the diegesis) has been emptied of the sequences of *apparently* diverse and novel events that fill most of the stories. From a this-worldly perspective, the woman's days look deceptively like pure repetition, as the imperfect tense here indicates. The mortal world then reasserts its claims. Events get underway again, and the preterite returns, as a French army ship rescues the wife ('les gens qui estoient dedans *aviserent* [...]'; 'The crew [caught] sight [...]'; p. 551; **67**: p. 504). This perhaps mirrors what would have happened to the interlocutors had *L'Heptaméron* been completed: presumably they would have returned from the 'desert' to their usual lives, whether or not they had travelled any spiritual distance towards mortification.

Many other novellas similarly tell of protagonists, especially women, who are trapped, imprisoned, confined, literally or metaphorically or both, usually by or on behalf of men, whether husbands, fathers, brothers, lovers or friars. Indeed, perhaps no other work from the period analyses so profoundly how the mortal world's power structures favour men over women. Whereas the woman stranded on the island in Novella 67 can do nothing to escape, other women face ethical dilemmas as to whether rebellion against men who have familial, economic, political or institutional power over them amounts to obedience or disobedience to the 'other world' to which they owe their ultimate allegiance. As the rebellious Rolandine says in Novella 21, however unjust my earthly father, 'I have another in heaven' (p. 267). But overall, as the inter-locutors' disagreements about the protagonists' behaviour show, *L'Heptaméron* offers no foolproof formula for distinguishing between the claims of the human world and the 'other world'.

Selected reading

Texts

64. Jean Calvin, *Oeuvres choisies*, ed. O. Millet (Paris, 1995). Contains Bible prefaces, the treatise on relics and other works.
65. ———, *Three French Treatises*, ed. F. Higman (London, 1970). Contains treatises on relics, the Eucharist and 'Nicodemites'. In French.
66. Marguerite de Navarre, *L'Heptaméron*, ed. N. Cazauran (Paris, 2000).
67. ———, *The Heptameron*, tr. P. Chilton (Harmondsworth, 1984).
68. Pierre de Ronsard, *Les Discours des misères de ce temps*, ed. M. Smith (Geneva, 1979). Ronsard's anti-Protestant poems.

Studies

Agrippa D'Aubigné

69. F. Lestringant, *Agrippa D'Aubigné: 'Les Tragiques'* (Paris, 1986). Introductory.

Marguerite de Navarre

70. J.D. Lyons and M. McKinley (eds), *Critical Tales: New Studies of the 'Heptameron' and Early Modern Culture* (Philadelphia, 1993).

5

'When I'm absent from you ...':
Lovers and Others

Gestures towards a spiritual 'other world' represented longing for God's full presence. They presupposed a degree of absence, during our mortal existence, of what matters to us most. The association between absence and desire was habitual. So D'Aubigné attempted to describe the indescribable (his future union with God) by inverting that association, envisaging 'hauts desirs sans absence' ('lofty desires devoid of absence'; **53**: vii, l. 1207). The phrase would have struck readers as strangely oxymoronic (an oxymoron juxtaposes contradictory or incongruous words).

Humanists longed not only (like others) for the presence of God, but also for that of classical antiquity, in the absence and shadow of which they wrote. Just as D'Aubigné imagined God's absence being overcome, so humanists in their most optimistic moments imagined antiquity's absence being overcome. Du Bellay, for example, lamenting the language barriers that impeded straightforward transmission of ancient knowledge to his generation, insists that language really should transmit such knowledge,

> affin que presens, absens, vyfz, et mors, manifestans l'un à l'autre le secret de notz coeurs, plus facilement parvenions à notre propre felicité, qui gist en l'intelligence des Sciences [...] (**22**: p. 103)

> so that present, absent, alive, or dead, communicating to one another the secrets of our hearts, we may more easily achieve happiness, which lies in the understanding of knowledge [...] (**23**: p. 56)

By communicating across generations, language ought to be able to conquer absence and death, or (in Thomas Greene's words) to 'pierce' a little the darkness of history' and 'relieve to a degree the solitude of a belated culture' (**60**: p. 191).

Heaven and antiquity were not the only entities whose absence provoked prolonged expressions of desire. Others included places in the contemporary world, especially homelands from which the writer-figure was exiled. For example, Joachim Du Bellay was in Rome from 1553 to 1557 running the household of his cousin Jean Du Bellay, ambassador to the Vatican. While there, Joachim wrote most of the sonnets of his 1558 *Regrets* (*Longings*). His poetic persona longs for France and his ancestral lands of Anjou, especially in the elegiac first third of the cycle. (The next third focuses more on satire of current Rome, and the final third on the initially disappointing return to France.) Through imitation of Ovid's poems of exile (the *Tristia* and the *Epistulae ex Ponto*), which are particularly prominent in this rich intertextual mix, the poet constructs an image of himself as involuntarily exiled, as wasting his life, far from where he could find success, wealth, happiness and love. The Ovidian epistle from exile had earlier been imitated by Clément Marot, for example, in his 'Epistre au Roy, du temps de son exil à Ferrare' ('Letter to the King from exile in Ferrara'; **14**: ii, pp. 80-6), written in 1535 after Marot, fearing for his safety in the backlash after the 1534 Affair of the Placards, had fled to courts more open to reform, first that of Marguerite de Navarre, then that of Ferrara.

The absence of particular people was lamented even more abundantly than that of places. The feeling of absence was profoundly inflected by the period's mentalities and technologies. For example, it was gendered in specific ways. Or, whereas nowadays we can hear, talk to, even see in real time (an electronic representation of) a loved one who is located miles away, in the sixteenth century physical absence meant abrupt cessation of any such sense-based communication and reciprocal simultaneity. On the other hand, educated people had perhaps a more explicit framework than do their twenty-first-century counterparts for describing how the mind compensates for such disuse of the external senses – through the operations of various faculties or *internal* senses. One of them, imagination, was considered to rework external sense data into images (not necessarily truthful ones) of absent objects such as loved ones, as well as of present objects. (The dominant framework that described this mental process and others was faculty psychology. It derived from scholasticism, and thus ultimately from Aristotle.)

Imagination was one compensation for absence. Imaginative writing was another, as we saw with D'Aubigné. A vast literature imagined ways of overcoming absence that separated people. Another historical specificity was a tension in such writing between, on the one hand, a conventional antithesis (absence versus presence) and, on the other hand, a tendency for that antithesis to break down, perhaps echoing more complex emotional and psychological realities in which presence and absence were bafflingly intertwined.

The bond was often homosocial (between people of the same sex) in one way or another. For example, Rabelais's Gargantua resorts to the period's most widely practised genre for overcoming physical absence – the letter – when writing to his son Pantagruel. Moreover, Gargantua imagines that their bodily bond will overcome even the more radical absence that will be introduced when he relocates to the 'other world':

> quand […] mon âme laissera cette habitation humaine, je ne me réputerai totalement mourir, ains passer d'un lieu en autre, attendu que en toi et par toi je demeure en mon image visible *en ce monde*, vivant, voyant, et conversant entre gens de honneur et mes amis comme je soulois […] (**29**: pp. 343-5)

> when my soul shall leave this human habitation, I shall not account myself to be totally dying, but passing from one place to another, considering that in you and through you I remain in my visible image *in this world*, living, seeing, and frequenting honourable people and my friends as I used to […] (**30**: p. 159)

This optimistic vision contrasts with, for example, Montaigne's description of his friendship with the dead La Boétie (i.27, 'De l'amitié'). The bond is again homosocial – in this case man-to-man friendship – but now it is replaced mainly by a grief-inducing void of absence.

5.1. Male-authored love poetry

The desire which absence was described as producing or exacerbating was very often overtly sexual. If homosexual, as it was in many ancient texts, it was usually condemned or reworked by humanist culture, as Guy Poirier has shown in a study that has opened up a new research field within sixteenth-century French studies (**77**). By contrast, heterosexual literature enjoyed enormous cultural visibility. Abundant love poetry, written largely by the male gentry, routinely yearned for the woman's physical presence. Despite her physical absence, the yearning may make her present in the mind of poet and reader. But even if she is physically present, she may still be absent in the sense of being an object of unfulfilled desire. These formulaic paradoxes, together with many others, belonged to a code of conventions known as Petrarchism. They derived from the vernacular love poetry of the Italian Petrarch.

Petrarch's *Canzoniere* (1347) expresses an unconsummated love for a woman, Laura, which continues beyond her death. Many features of this cycle were widely imitated by subsequent poets throughout Europe, especially in the sixteenth and seventeenth centuries. Poets seized especially on Petrarch's paradoxes, antitheses and oxymora, systematizing them further. The woman is absent and present, kind and cruel, friendly and disdainful. The poet is living and dead, hot (with love) and cold (with fear), free and captive, and so on. Despite its apparent rigidity, the Petrarchist code was used in many different ways. In Leonard Forster's words, it formed 'the second great international system of conventional love, between the chivalric love of the middle ages and the romantic love of the eighteenth and nineteenth centuries' (**80**: p. 2).

French love poetry was steeped in Petrarchism, particularly in the second half of the sixteenth century. The very notion of addressing a cycle of poems to one female figure was Petrarchist. Du Bellay produced one of the first two such cycles of French sonnets (*L'Olive*, 1549) but satirized Petrarchism in the mid-1550s ('Contre les pétrarquistes', **74**: pp. 70-82). Ronsard imitated Petrarchism especially in two of the sonnet sequences he addressed largely to a single figure – Cassandre (*Amours*, 1552 and 1553) and Hélène (*Sonets pour Helene*, 1578). Yet he also undermined Petrarchism in both, whether through aggressive eroticism in the *Amours* (mediated through imitation of Latin love poetry) or through ironic detachment in the *Sonets pour Helene*.

5.1.1. Maurice Scève, 'Délie'

The Lyon poet Scève chose not sonnets but dizains (ten-line poems) for his sequence *Délie* (1544). Scève's poetic persona is less assertive and more melancholic than that often adopted by Ronsard. In this respect it is closer to Petrarch's. The stock absence/presence antithesis often dominates:

> Étant ainsi veuve de sa présence,
> Je l'ay si vive en mon intention,
> Que je la vois toute telle en absence,
> Qu'elle est au lieu de sa détention.   4
> Par divers acte et mainte invention,
> Je la contemple en pensée rassise.
> Ci elle allait, là elle était assise,
> Ici tremblant lui fis mes doléances,   8
> En cette part une sienne devise
> Me reverdit mes mortes espérances. (Dizain 363)

Bereaved as I am of her presence, I have her so vivid in my mind that, even in her absence, I see her wholly as she is in the place where she is held captive. Through various mental processes and techniques, in calm thought I gaze upon her. Here she walked and there she sat; here, trembling, I told her my anguish and in that place something she said revived my dead hopes.

The rich opening rhyme describes Délie as both absent (l. 3) and not present (l. 1). The inner eye of the poet's mind can still see her, but he cautiously stops short of claiming that she is therefore present in a sense. So he nuances the commonplace that the woman is present to the man's mind even when bodily absent. Nonetheless, the poem does initially suggest that his mental image miraculously captures a present reality, even that of a place – Délie's prison-like marital home – to which the poet's *external* senses have no access. He reinforces the suggestion through the rhetorical figure of hyperbole ('toute telle'), hammered home by the 't'-'t'-'t' alliteration and the assertive present indicative ('elle est'). The 'v'-'v' alliteration of 'vive' (l. 2) counters that of 'veuve' (l. 1), compensating for the emptiness resulting from the loss of her bodily presence with the plenitude ('toute telle') of a mental picture whose visual sharpness is then emphasized still more by the echoing 'v' of 'vois' in the next line (l. 3). '[V]ois' echoes 'vive' all the more strongly because each comes just before the caesura, that is, on the fourth syllable of the decasyllabic line, which also means that the line's rhythm gives them major stress.

However, the lover's clear, certain, mental image then becomes blurred. Having started as an imagination of what Délie is doing now, in his bodily absence, it becomes a memory of what she did in the past, in his bodily presence. The tense shifts from the present to the imperfect (l. 7) and the past historic (ll. 8, 10). These past tenses render less immediate any presence that she may have now in his mind. Even his near-oxymoronic, Petrarchist 'mortes esperances' were revived only in the past. The particular past tense selected (the past historic rather than the

perfect) suggests that the revival is not necessarily continuing now. Moreover, the shift from present to past tenses is not explained or announced. It surprises the reader. This is characteristic of Scève's dense decasyllabic dizains which, in comparison with, say, sonnets in alexandrines, often dispense with explanatory links such as conjunctive phrases, sometimes creating the impression of a mind not in complete rational control of its thought-flow. Here, the way in which imagination tapers off into memory suggests that the supposedly truthful imagination of Délie in her invisible home was in fact concocted out of memories of her in other places. What she is actually like in her home perhaps remains inaccessible to him.

On the other hand, even if memory here lacks the immediacy of vivid imagination, at least it gives a representation of the absent beloved that is more grounded in reality. Or does it? Syntactical ambiguity, another characteristic of Scève's dense style, makes it unclear whether the person immersed in their thoughts in line 6 is him now (the more likely sense, with 'rassise' agreeing with 'pensée') or her then (with 'rassise' referring to her). Although line 5 probably refers to him now, it could also conceivably refer to her then. These ambiguities tarnish the clarity of her presence in his mind. It is uncertain exactly where the remembering subject ends and the remembered object begins. Indeed, this uncertainty grows out of the more general oscillation between him (ll. 6, 8) and her (ll. 7, 9) as the grammatical subject during the reminiscing.

This is a poem of absence, lit up by flashes of possible presence. The opening antithesis between presence and absence ends up being compromised and complicated. By drawing attention, here and elsewhere, to failures in a male representation of a woman, Scève perhaps reflects more explicitly than most other male love poets on ways in which the woman they apparently describe is, in one sense, entirely absent, precisely because in the poem she becomes an object – desired, gazed upon, descriptively dissected (e.g. **31**: i, p. 449, Sonnet 12), having no autonomy or agency beyond the erotic and emotional impact which he claims she has on him.

5.2. Women on love

Many male poets wove Petrarchism together with neo-Platonism in ways that make the female object a passport to presence, rather than a presence in her own right. The erotic love described in Plato's *Symposium* was homosexual to a considerable degree, as also in Ficino (although he downplayed physical sex), whereas French writers made it heterosexual. Through the neo-Platonic frenzies (*fureurs*) of love and poetry, adoring a woman's mortal beauty was a way for the male poet's soul to rejoin the World Soul, to reach the realm of the Ideas, or, as Ronsard put it in Sonnet 172 of the *Amours*, 'pour adorer là haut / L'autre beauté dont la tienne est venue' ('to adore on high the other beauty from which your own has come'; **31**: i, p. 115; **32**: p. 20).

Sometimes, however, the supposed objects talked back. A few women, such as Marguerite de Navarre, Labé, Pernette Du Guillet (*Rymes*, 1545), Catherine des Roches and Helisenne de Crenne, managed to get *their* writing about love into print. They imitated the frameworks of Petrarchism and/or neo-Platonism yet disturbed them from within. Some used neo-Platonism to encourage men to behave respectfully and chastely towards the women they claimed to love, rather than just angling to have sex with them (e.g. **66**: pp. 242-3). Catherine des Roches goes further still in an anti-neo-Platonist prose dialogue. Charité refuses to be turned into a passport to both pleasure and metaphysical presence. She satirizes her suitor Sincero's double entendre request to take him to heaven:

> Si n'ay-je point souvenance d'y avoir jamais esté; mais possible m'en ferez-vous revenir la memoire me disant ce que j'aperceu de plus esmerveillable en ce voyage. (**19**: pp. 57-8, 253)

Yet I can't recall ever having been there. But perhaps you'll jog my memory by telling me what the most amazing things were that I saw on the trip.

5.2.1. Louise Labé

Neo-Platonism is reworked in more sombre tones by Labé's Sonnet 22:

> Luisant Soleil, que tu es bien heureus,
> De voir tousjours de t'Amie la face:
> Et toy, sa seur, qu'Endimion embrasse,
> Tant te repais de miel amoureus.   4
>
> Mars voit Venus: Mercure aventureus
> De Ciel en Ciel, de lieu en lieu se glasse:
> Et Jupiter remarque en mainte place
> Ses premiers ans plus gays et chaleureus.   8
>
> Voilà du Ciel la puissante harmonie,
> Qui les esprits divins ensemble lie:
> Mais s'ils avoient ce qu'ils ayment lointein,   11
>
> Leur harmonie et ordre irrevocable
> Se tourneroit en erreur variable,
> Et comme moy travailleroient en vain.   14

Radiant sun, how very fortunate you are to see your lover's face all the time. And you, the sun's sister, kissed by Endymion, how you feed on love's honey! Mars sees Venus. Intrepid Mercury glides from one heavenly sphere to another, from one place to another. And Jupiter perceives in many locations the fruits of his early, friskier, and steamier years. So there, in all of that, lies the

powerful harmony of the heavens, which binds divine spirits
together. But if what they love was far from them, then their
harmony and unbreakable order would turn into inconsistent,
erratic, erroneous wandering, and they would suffer uselessly, as I
do.

As François Rigolot and others have observed, this sonnet plays
with Ficino's theory that Love produces harmony throughout the
cosmos (**27**: p. 24). In a sense, the theory is largely confirmed here.
But it is drained of force, since the sole exception to it – the poet's
experience – is what actually matters. The sonnet ends, like many
in the period, with a *pointe* – a twist or memorable expression. Only
in the final line does the first-person speaker refer to herself
('comme moy'). And only then do we realize that the purpose of the
first ten lines is to convey something (her pain) that is the opposite
of what they describe (cosmic bliss). The solitude produced by her
lover's absence is compounded by her not fitting in with the
universe. In Chapter 6 we will encounter the great neo-Platonic
mapping of macrocosm onto microcosm. But here it comes unstuck.
Instead of being plugged into the cosmos, the poet is a jarring, dwin-
dling detail, as is suggested by the thin closing rhyme
('lointein'/'vain'), the only 'poor' one in the poem. Even the poet's
sex is not stated.

By contrast, the quatrains apparently describe a plenitude of
presence, dependent on the external senses of sight (ll. 2, 5, 7),
touch, and taste (ll. 3-4). But perhaps even this description already
dimly foreshadows a female's imminent discomfort within the
cosmos. The hierarchical 'order' of the planet-gods is gendered (as
it was in the period's cosmological theories). Males (Mars, Jupiter
and the sun-god, who is Apollo or Helios) do the active seeing,
while females (Selene the moon-god and Venus) are seen.
Moreover, although he is not a god, it is the eternally sleeping
male Endymion who does the kissing, not his divine partner
Selene. The only two protagonists not mentioned by name –
Clytia (who is probably the 'Amie' of line 2) and the moon (Selene,

sister of Helios, in line 3) – are both female, anticipating the female poet's own anonymity in line 14. Moreover, beneath the male bliss described by lines 1-2 there lies a story of female suffering: the reason why Apollo always sees Clytia's face is that this distraught water nymph changed into a sunflower after staring for days at the sun-god after he had jilted her (Ovid, *Metamorphoses*, IV: 206-70).

In other poems, Labé reworks masculine discourses in rather different directions, amplifying female desire for the male lover's bodily presence – a startling inversion of usual roles. She vividly appropriates Petrarchism's standard scenarios for envisaging sexual union – dream and fantasy (Sonnets 9 and 13). She uses the concrete verb *acoller* ('put one's arms around someone's neck') twice in Sonnet 13 to imagine such body-to-body presence.

Three years earlier, in 1552, Ronsard had used the same verb in an even more sexually explicit dream of such presence: 'Quand en songeant ma follastre j'accole, [...] / En sa moitié ma moitié je recole' ('When, in my dreams, I put my arms around my sexy lover's neck, I glue my half back into hers'; **31**: i, p. 465). He reduces here to its physical dimension the Platonic myth of the Androgynes, the man-woman creatures that Zeus split in two. Although that dimension was powerful in Plato's account (*Symposium*, 189c-), the myth was interpreted as describing a mainly spiritual reconnecting between men and women by others such as Antoine Héroet, whose verse 'Androgyne de Platon', composed in 1536, was based on Ficino's Latin translation of the *Symposium* (**26**: pp. 71-89).

5.2.2. Helisenne de Crenne

One female writer used the genre of the prose *roman* (romance) to explore desire for a particular man's bodily presence. Marguerite Briet de Crenne wrote under the partial pseudonym Helisenne de Crenne. In Book 1 of her *Angoysses douloureuses qui procedent d'amours* (*The Torments to which Love Leads*, 1538), the first-person narrator, who is also called Helisenne, recounts how, some time ago, she married very young, then fell in love with a man called Guenelic; how the lovers managed to exchange a few words and letters; and how Helisenne's irate husband then kept them apart by imprisoning her in the castle of Cabasus. Book 2 is apparently narrated by Guenelic, although in fact, all his words (we are told) are imagined by the narrator Helisenne. This ventriloquized voice of Guenelic relates how he and his male friend Quezinstra searched for Helisenne through many lands, and (in Book 3) how they at last found Helisenne, tried to free her, but were discovered; how Guenelic and Quezinstra, leaving Helisenne on her own while they repelled her captors, returned only to find Helisenne dying from anxiety and grief at what she thought would be Guenelic's death and eternal 'absence' (**72**: p. 464); how Guenelic in turn then died of grief. Guenelic's death creates a problem, since he is supposedly doing the retrospective narrating, but cannot carry on with the story after the point in it at which he has died. So the narrating is now taken over by Quezinstra. He recounts how the gods' messenger Mercury then appeared and took away the two lovers' souls to the kingdom of Minos. There they were adjudged worthy of going to the Elysian Fields (that is, pagan heaven).

On many levels, this fiction describes a quest for presence. Indeed, the terms 'presence' and 'absence' recur throughout. Guenelic's physical presence has an overwhelming effect on Helisenne. It is variously described, by the narrator and other protagonists, as inflaming, endangering or restoring her. Indeed, it is what makes her fall in love with him, although she has never spoken to him. Presence in this context involves the external senses. It mainly means his being within her sight, but also within her hearing, when he sings to her invisibly from the street. But such moments are rare. So, like Scève's poet-lover, she creates in her imagination and memory, and once in dream, a simulacrum of her beloved's presence (pp. 105, 109, 188). However, like Scève, Crenne the author complicates this commonplace. Her narrator-protagonist Helisenne worries that the simulacrum might be what she is in love with (pp. 188-9, 201). This anxiety is deepened, but her love not lessened, by incipient signs of Guenelic's unworthy character. These strike a discordant note relative to the chivalric-romance genre that Crenne is mainly adapting.

That narrative genre, combined with others, such as the exemplary tale, also enables Crenne to explore social and textual dimensions of presence and absence more extensively than love poets could. Helisenne's husband is frequently described as someone who is either menacingly present or blessedly absent. Moreover, even before he locks her away in the castle, he has the most power over the spatial chess game of absence and presence, like countless real and fictional husbands of the period. He tells Helisenne:

> Je vous prohibe et deffendz de vous trouver en lieu ou il [Guenelic] soyt en mon absence, et oultreplus quand je seroye present, et feust à l'elevation du corps de Jesuchrist, je veulx que incontinent que vous le pourrez percepvoir que sans dilation vous absentez [...] (p. 125)

> I absolutely forbid you to be in the same place as him [Guenelic] in my absence; and even when I am present, if you should spot him, then I want you to absent yourself immediately, even if it's at Mass at the moment when the priest lifts up Christ's body.

Unlike Helisenne, the men – both the husband and Guenelic (who roams in search of her in Book 2) – are able to move freely through many places.

Since space is structured by gender, so is absence. This is apparent not only in the fictions of Crenne and Marguerite de Navarre but in numerous other kinds of writing. For example, both Catherine and Madeleine Des Roches sometimes composed poems in which they adopted the persona of a woman who was far from her lover or husband. One of these was written to order for a noblewoman whose husband was in Constantinople for five years as French ambassador: as almost always in sixteenth-century life and literature, it is the man who roams through space while the woman is at home. One might therefore expect *him* to be described as absent. And yet the *woman* is, in the first line of this poem and another like it: 'Absente de vos yeux' ('Absent from your eyes'); 'Quand je suis de vous absente [...]' ('When I'm absent from you [...]'; **73**: p. 134; **19**: p.281). Since in the period's dominant discourses women's social identity is more dependent than men's on their opposite-sex partner, when men go away then women's identity threatens to do so too. Women can become 'absent' without moving an inch.

Since women's movements were more restricted than men's, writing was sometimes even more crucial to them as one of the few available means of trying to overcome absence. A real-life example is Jeanne Boulet, Baroness of Germoles, who paid Catherine Des Roches to write that poem in her voice, urging her husband to return from Constantinople and to not stray sexually. The poem was printed in a collection of model missives, in prose and verse (*Les Missives*, 1586). Such collections by women were rare. The first was published by Marguerite Briet under her semi-fictional persona of Helisenne de Crenne (*Les Epistres familieres et invectives*, 1539). Imitating in her own way the traditions of the *ars dictaminis*, Erasmus and Cicero's *Ad familiares*, she explores the imagination, conjecture and anxiety that are produced by separation combined with restricted travel possibilities, for example in the third letter, addressed to a female relative. A fictional example that was probably rooted in real-life events is Novella 22 in Marguerite de Navarre's *L'Heptaméron*. A young confined nun, Marie Héroet (from the same family as the neo-Platonizing Antoine) passes secretly to her visiting brother a written account of the sexual harassment she has suffered. This exposes the perpetrator.

Yet another fictional example of female writing overcoming absence, which may or may not have roots in Marguerite Briet's own life, is *Les Angoysses douloureuses* itself. The narrator-protagonist Helisenne writes an account of her husband's cruelty towards her. But her husband burns it, so she reconstructs it in her memory and writes it out again in her prison, believing that all her troubles will cease if ever she can transmit it to Guenelic (**72**: p. 218). She never does. However, her handwritten account does eventually overcome her isolation in ways she has not anticipated, because Mercury finds the manuscript by her dead body (p. 489). After being reunited with Guenelic and hearing of his wanderings, Helisenne had added to the manuscript an account of those wanderings (in Guenelic's voice). Now, after her death, her manuscript gets printed: Mercury takes it to the gods; Pallas (Minerva) and Venus argue over its meaning; Jupiter orders it to be printed in Paris as a warning of what torments love brings. So the book we have just read corresponds exactly to what the protagonist herself wrote (except for Quezinstra's closing narrative of events after her death).

The book is therefore represented as communicating with everyone – both within and beyond the diegesis – except the person (Guenelic) for whom it was initially intended. It ends up being used as a caution against precisely the kind of union that the narrator-protagonist Helisenne tried to bring about in writing it. This ambivalence is ultimately irreducible, since *Les Angoysses douloureuses* is both a warning against, and a celebration of, sensual love. The immortal 'other world' provides various kinds of presence that were impossible in the mortal world: not only are the lovers reunited but their souls are saved and will be permanently re-joined to their bodies (p. 495). Perhaps only by representing the afterlife in terms of pagan mythology (a culmination of the work's strong humanist strand) can Crenne the author bring off this uneasy coexistence between an apotheosis and condemnation of the lovers. Whether they would have been allowed into a Christian heaven remains an open question.

Love, for humans and/or for God, was not the only desire represented as a kind of reaching out towards eternal presence from within the everyday. The same went for attempts to understand nature, as we shall now see.

Selected reading

Texts

71. Helisenne de Crenne, *Les Epistres familieres et invectives*, ed. J. Nash (Paris, 1996).
72. ———, *Les Angoysses douloureuses qui procedent d'amours*, ed. C. de Buzon (Paris, 1997). There is also a paperback edition by J.-P. Beaulieu, Saint-Étienne, 2005.
73. Madeleine Des Roches and Catherine Des Roches, *Les Missives*, ed. A. Larsen (Geneva, 1999).
74. Joachim Du Bellay, *Divers jeux rustiques*, ed. V.L. Saulnier (Paris and Geneva, 1965).
75. ———, *Les Regrets, suivi de: Les Antiquités de Rome, Le Songe*, ed. F. Roudaut (Paris, 2002).
76. Maurice Scève, *Délie*, ed. F. Charpentier (Paris, 1984).

Studies

77. G. Poirier, *L'Homosexualité dans l'imaginaire de la Renaissance* (Paris, 1996).

*Love poetry (see also **60**: ch. 10 on Ronsard's Amours)*

78. T. Cave (ed.), *Ronsard the Poet* (London, 1973). On the full range of Ronsard's poetry, not just love. Considers Petrarchism, neo-Platonism, mythology and so on.
79. D. Coleman, *Maurice Scève, Poet of Love: Tradition and Originality* (Cambridge, 1975).
80. L. Forster, *The Icy Fire: Five Studies in European Petrarchism* (Cambridge, 1969). Chapter 1 outlines Petrarchist conventions.

81. A.R. Jones, *The Currency of Eros: Women's Love Lyric in Europe, 1540-1620* (Bloomington and Indianapolis, 1990). Sections on Catherine Des Roches, Du Guillet and Labé.

Helisenne de Crenne

82. J.-P. Beaulieu and D. Desrosiers-Bonin (eds), *Hélisenne de Crenne: L'Écriture et ses doubles* (Paris, 2004). On all her works. Advanced.

6

'Until I ... go to see that beautiful place': Hidden Recesses of Nature, the Cosmos, the Future

6.1. Elements, humours, soul, planets

People also imagined and tried to know those invisible or semi-visible places and structures that lie within nature and the cosmos but largely beyond the reach of the external senses. And those places were sometimes believed to give access to a time, one that is hidden even more than the past: the future.

People imagined such hidden realities by extrapolating from what they *could* see, touch, hear and so on. For most people, but especially the educated, the extrapolating was shaped by certain ancient texts. Indeed, in sixteenth-century epistemology (theory of knowledge), one of the three major routes to knowledge was authority (that is, texts deemed to be authoritative). The other two routes were experience (particular data, provided by the external senses) and reason (which produced universal conclusions, often from that data). Yet even epistemological optimists thought that they would not gain full knowledge of all times and places until they entered the 'other world' of heaven.

People believed – as do we now for different reasons – that our immediate physical environment is merely a surface, beneath which more intangible realities lurk. Some of these realities were meta-physical, that is, underlying structures of being that are separable from matter. Others were physical. The period's dominant physics, like its metaphysics, was still broadly scholastic and Aristotelian. It posited the existence of four elements: fire, air, water and earth (in descending order of weight and nobility). Everything in nature, that is, everything sub-lunar (beneath the moon) is composed of a changing, unequal mixture of these four elements. So the elements are distinct from what in everyday experience we call fire, air, water and earth. For example, the water we drink is actually a mixture of all four elements, dominated however, by the element water. So our senses of sight, taste, and so on only give us partial access to the elements, which we never experience in their pure, unmixed state.

According to this dominant Aristotelian framework, elements have qualities, which are of two kinds: active and occult. Only the active ones are 'sensible' (capable of being perceived by external senses): they can be touched. There are four of these active qualities: hotness, coldness, moistness and dryness. Each element possesses two of them:

Element	Qualities	Humour	Temperament
fire	hot/dry	yellow bile	choleric
air	hot/moist	blood	sanguine
water	cold/moist	phlegm	phlegmatic
earth	cold/dry	black bile	melancholic

The sub-lunar world is in constant flux, because elements fight with each other via their contrary qualities – rain, which is mainly cold and moist, extinguishes flames, which are mainly hot and dry. And the elements change into each other by exchanging qualities – rain evaporates, turning into air, keeping much of its moistness but swapping much of its coldness for hotness. As for occult qualities, they lie beyond our external senses: only reason tells us that they exist. They explain otherwise inexplicable sympathies and antipathies, such as the attraction of magnet to metal.

Reason suggested that specific kinds of intangible recesses lurk within the human body. This was assumed for example by humoral theory, which derived from ancient Greek medicine, especially from the physiology that Galen had grafted onto Aristotelian physics – see the table above. (Galen remained the dominant authority in medicine, despite increasing challenges, for instance from the modern Swiss physician Paracelsus [1493-1541] – supported by some in France from the 1560s – and also from new knowledge derived from dissection of humans by the Flemish anatomist Andreas Vesalius [1514-64] and others; Galen had only dissected animals.)

Galenic theory held that the body is kept alive by four humours – black bile, phlegm, blood and yellow bile. These are the 'real bodily fluids' that our senses perceive; and yet humoral theory also ascribed to them 'largely hypothetical origins, sites, and functions' (**89**: p. 105). It held, for instance, that a person's temperament is determined by his or her characteristic mixture of humours, in which one humour is dominant (see the table above). But if the mixture becomes too uneven, or if humours burn or putrefy, then illness ensues. The humours are produced by the liver when it cooks 'chyle' (a substance that the stomach has made out of food). Once the humours have been produced, they keep us alive by spreading heat throughout the body, via three kinds of 'spirit' (vital, natural and animal).

Invisible functions were also attributed to these 'spirits'. The functions overlapped to some extent with those attributed to soul, since soul (*anima* in Latin) was considered to be what animates us (and all living things). The operations of soul, while even less accessible to sight, touch and so on than the operations of the elements and humours, were similarly extrapolated from what *could* be empirically perceived. With soul, as with physics, the dominant theory remained Aristotelian and scholastic, despite the new prominence of the very different neo-Platonic theory encountered above.

In scholastic faculty psychology (derived from Aristotle's *On the Soul*), the soul has three faculties: vegetative, sensitive and intellective. Humans have all three; animals have vegetative and sensitive; plants have only vegetative. First, vegetative soul, whether in plants, animals or humans, involves powers of nutrition, growth and procreation. Secondly, sensitive soul, whether in animals or humans, involves sensation, movement, desire and limited powers of cogitation – basically, everything animals can do but plants cannot. It includes the external senses (taste, hearing, and so on), as well as internal ones, one of which was discussed earlier (imagination). Thirdly, intellective soul, which is found only in humans, involves reasoning, willing and memorizing abstract concepts – basically, whatever humans can do that animals (supposedly) cannot. In scholasticism's Christianized development of Aristotle, intellective soul is immortal, detachable from the body, and so cannot be perceived by sight, touch, and so on. On the other hand, the powers of the two other faculties of soul, vegetative and sensitive, are partly observable through the body's operations.

By contrast, Ficinian neo-Platonism tended to separate body from soul more sharply. Although soul inhabits our body – in which a fragment of World Soul is temporarily imprisoned – and communicates with our body through a tenuously material substance called spirit, nonetheless, in Ficino's hierarchy of being, soul is a cut-off point: above it, reality becomes purely immaterial, eternal.

Such higher reaches of reality and remote recesses of the cosmos were variously imagined by people, again on the basis of what they *could* see – which was not very much. As in physics, physiology and faculty psychology, so in cosmology the most widely held basic tenets remained largely unchanged from the medieval period. They were a Christianized and simplified version of what the Greek astronomer Ptolemy had outlined 14 centuries earlier, refining Aristotle. In this view, the cosmos is spherical, finite and geocentric (that is, with the earth at its centre). Near the outer rim of the universe is a sphere of fixed stars (the asterisks in the diagram on p. 00). Between the fixed stars and the Earth are other invisible spheres, upon which the seven planets are embedded (in ascending order: the moon, Mercury, Venus, the sun, Mars, Jupiter and Saturn). These spheres are not geometrical abstractions, but are made of crystal and fill the vastness of space – there is no such thing as a vacuum.

This Ptolemaic system lasted so long because it seemed to extrapolate plausibly from the little that *could* be seen in this period before telescopes (which were invented in the early seventeenth century). The naked eye could see seven planets, whose movements could be measured by various instruments known as astrolabes. In order to make his theory fit in with what could be observed (and so 'save the appearances') Ptolemy had accounted for visible irregularities in the planets' orbits around Earth by postulating a secondary level of mini-orbits (epicycles) that planets make within their main sphere. Another extrapolation that seemed plausible on the basis of what the eye could see was a sharp distinction between the sub-lunar and supra-lunar realms. Whereas all is flux beneath the moon – where, in the diagram, the four elements can be seen – above the moon there is perfect stability. According to Aristotle, this supra-lunar realm is made of a single fifth element (quintessence), called aether.

Christians added details of their own to the outer, most remote reaches of the Ptolemaic cosmos, locating there the divine 'other world' we encountered in Chapter 4. Beyond the sphere of the fixed stars, they placed at least one more sphere, calling it the 'prime mover' ('Premier mouvant' in the diagram), since it sets in motion the other spheres. Beyond it they located the highest heaven or empyrean ('Ciel empire' in the diagram), where God and the elect dwell. Unlike the spheres, which are circumscribed, it extends out into infinity.

6.2. Occult philosophy: magic, astrology, divination

Not everyone imagined the secret places and structures of the world in the same way, however. These dominant views were not ubiquitous. Indeed, humanism unsettled what we would nowadays roughly call 'science' and what was known in the period rather as 'natural philosophy' and as philosophy of a 'speculative' or theoretical kind. ('Philosophy', although defined in various ways, roughly covered everything knowable by human reason. It also encompassed 'practical' or 'active' areas such as moral life – as we saw earlier – and politics.) Humanists injected a bewildering choice into speculative as well as moral philosophy. They revived a range of ancient theories of physics and metaphysics which now competed with scholasticism: not only Platonism and neo-Platonism, but also Stoicism and Epicureanism, for example. Neo-Platonists also promoted a body of part-philosophical religious writings that they (wrongly) believed to be *extremely* ancient, dating from just after Moses' time. They thought that this 'Hermetic Corpus' had been composed by the divinely inspired Hermes Trismegistus. They considered it to be at the start of a tradition of 'ancient theology' (*prisca theologia*).

These non-Aristotelian traditions provided alternative ways of imagining the relationship between our immediate physical surroundings and the remote recesses of the cosmos. Whereas in Aristotelianism the moon marks a radical discontinuity between the imperfect terrestrial realm and the perfect celestial one, on the other hand neo-Platonic and Hermetic writing described how the world down here, and especially the 'small world' (microcosm) of the human being – body, spirit and soul – is intricately connected to the 'large world' (macrocosm), that is, to the upper reaches of the cosmos. The mapping of microcosm onto macrocosm had also characterized some medieval thought. But many humanists now sought to both understand and exploit it better. Learned magic, astrology, divination and alchemy promised ways of doing that. Thanks to humanism, the more theoretically sophisticated varieties of occult philosophy enjoyed in the fifteenth and sixteenth centuries a heyday that – particularly in the case of magic, astrology and divination – has never been rivalled in the West, bar their flowering in late antiquity.

Nonetheless, erudite magic was certainly controversial, not least for the Church. Some humanists defended it as a way of manipulating hidden powers for good purposes. They often divided magic into three kinds: natural, spiritual and demonic. First, natural magic, the least controversial, involved manipulating the occult qualities that (as we saw above) were thought to inhere in objects. Second, spiritual magic involved, for neo-Platonists like Ficino, manipulating an impersonal essence called World Spirit. Third, demonic magic involved enlisting the help of demons; neo-Platonists believed that good demons are situated one rung down from good angels in the cosmic hierarchy of 'intelligences'. Critics of demonic magic argued that, despite the best intentions of the wise magical operator (magus), the demons who answer his call may in fact be bad ones, turning his white magic into black. Especially controversial too were the ceremonial dimensions – rituals, gestures, special objects, and so on – which some devotees of magic believed to be necessary for conjuring up demons or spirit.

The forces which erudite magic sought to manipulate (occult qualities, demons and spirit) were all considered to emanate from God's will, to be vehicles or media through which His will beams down from the higher, immaterial reaches of the cosmos to the physical world. On its way down, it passes through the planets. The ways in which the planets pass it on to the sub-lunar world, as 'influence', were described by astrology. Like other theories of the cosmos that we have encountered, astrological theory was produced by extrapolating from sensible, visible and tangible reality. For example, extrapolating from the sun's evidently warming and illuminating effect on us, astrologers posited the existence of many other *imperceptible* rays of light and heat, streaming down to Earth from each planet.

Learned astrology achieved considerable cultural prominence. For many centuries it had been based on Ptolemy and other ancient authorities (such as Firmicus Maternus), to whom Arabic ones had been added from the thirteenth century. And it had more recently been reinforced by the humanist rediscovery of the ancient Roman poet Manilius's long astrological poem. Learned astrology described how planetary influence is shaped partly by the 12 'houses' or segments (governing our wealth, career, and so on) into which the path of the sun's orbit (the ecliptic) is divided, and partly by the 12 constellations of the zodiac (the band round the ecliptic). (The constellations' symbols are shown in the diagram, within the eighth sphere.)

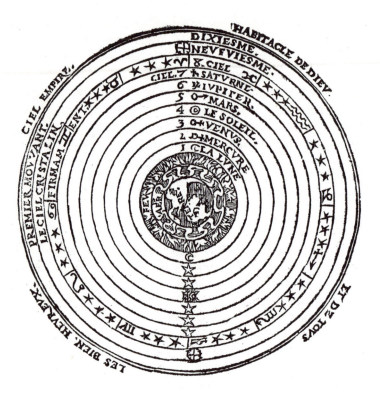

Peter Apian, *Cosmographia*, Paris, 1551, fol. 3r. Reproduced by
permission of the Syndics of Cambridge University Library.

There were essentially two kinds of astrology, natural and judicial.
Natural (or physical) astrology involved, for example, foretelling the
weather and natural catastrophes or else calculating the most effective
time for administering medical cures. On the other hand, judicial
astrology was much more controversial. It predicted what would
happen to people because of the influence of the stars (planets) on
them, as revealed by natal charts (horoscopes) and other means. It
also provided answers to those who sought lost property or wondered
exactly when it would be most propitious to undertake, say, a journey.

In judicial astrology, therefore, knowing the remote *places* of the cosmos was inseparable from knowing a remote *time* – the future. So judicial astrology was sometimes called divinatory astrology, and was just one of the many branches of the art generally known as divination. Divination was the art both of foretelling and also discovering certain kinds of secret knowledge. Although divination sought knowledge of things that lay well beyond the reach of the external senses, its starting-point was mostly what *could* be perceived by them. In other words, it consisted in interpreting various perceptible phenomena. Some of these were considered to be 'given' (*oblativa* in Latin) rather than instigated by humans: a flash of lightning, a flight of birds, and so on. Others, more controversial, were considered to be instigated by humans (*impetrativa*): the appearance of a chicken's entrails, the lie of dice, and so on. This distinction was transmitted by Cicero, whose *On Divination* and *On the Nature of the Gods* were the main sources of sixteenth-century knowledge of ancient divination. Cicero's typologies were sometimes reworked. For instance, the German Kaspar Peucer, whose 1553 treatise on divination was known in the French-speaking world, distinguished between phenomena which occur *ordinarily* in nature (planetary movements, the lines of someone's face) and others which do not ('monsters', such as conjoined twins). But whatever the typology adopted, divination treated such phenomena as omens, as signs to be interpreted. Although divination was often associated with magic, it was mostly speculative (concerned with finding things out), whereas magic was mostly operative (concerned with getting things done).

In these areas – natural philosophy, medicine and occult philosophy – the effervescence generated by humanism and other factors led in the sixteenth century and then especially the seventeenth to what has been labelled the 'Scientific Revolution'. A variety of frameworks gradually seemed to describe more plausibly (than, for example, scholasticism and much occult philosophy) the recesses of nature and of the cosmos. These frameworks were developed by Copernicus (1473-1543), Galileo (1564-1642), Kepler (1571-1630),

Descartes (1596-1650), Newton (1642-1727) and others, although often inspired by non-Aristotelian or even occult philosophy (Epicurus, Plato, Pythagoras, the Hermetic Corpus and so on). Aristotelian physics, which was qualititative in the sense of being based on qualities, was eventually replaced by quantitative approaches, which focused instead on measuring physical quantities mathematically. This enabled experimental method to be developed as a challenge to the traditional epistemological notions of experience and textual authority. Moreover, the distinction between terrestrial and celestial physics was increasingly undermined.

6.3. Writing in French: the example of divination

Written imagining of the hidden recesses of nature and the cosmos was still mostly done in Latin in sixteenth-century France. Moreover, such was the cosmopolitan humanist Republic of Letters that many French readers knew the major, sometimes controversial neo-Latin writings on speculative philosophy, astrology, magic and divination by the likes of the Germans Peucer and Heinrich Cornelius Agrippa von Nettesheim (1486-1535) or the Italians Ficino (1433-99), Giovanni Pico della Mirandola (1463-94) and Giambattista della Porta (*c.* 1535-1615).

However, it also became much more common to publish in *French* one's imaginings of these remote recesses. The stretching of the vernacular to incorporate technical discourses occurred in speculative philosophy as well as in theology, poetics and other areas. This use of French was partly motivated by a concern to popularize, extending the potential range of non-latinate readers who could gain some philosophical knowledge, which sometimes got simplified in the process. But vernacular writing was not just a passive vehicle for Latin philosophy: it re-worked, re-assessed and re-applied it in crucial ways.

Just about any French text from the period, whatever its topic, contains at least traces of these kinds of imagining of extra-sensible realities. Innumerable sonnets, letters, treatises, plays and histories refer in unsystematic ways to the elements, qualities, humours, spirits, planets, demons, and so on, just as Shakespeare does. At the opposite, systematic extreme are philosophical works such as the *Académie françoise* (*French Academy*, 1577-98) by the Calvinist Pierre de La Primaudaye. This moralizing prose encyclopaedia of all kinds of knowledge includes lengthy discussions of the body, nature and the cosmos.

As it made its way into the vernacular, speculative and occult philosophy was re-shaped by the range of genres and aims involved. Let us take the example of divination, beginning with judicial astrology. At the systematic end of the spectrum, Calvin sought to dissuade his flock from consulting judicial astrologers. For this he used a genre that we earlier saw him use against relics: the short polemical treatise, bordering on the pamphlet or sermon (**83**: p. 32). His *Advertissement contre l'astrologie qu'on appelle judiciaire* (1549) does not make a philosophical case. It does not undermine the premises of judicial astrology on that art's own, technical terrain, as Pico had done famously in 1495 (**83**: p. 15). Indeed, like most educated people, Calvin accepts astrological influence as a fact. And he has no problem with natural astrology. Rather, he argues on theological grounds. Judicial astrology seeks to pin down God's will, whereas God is free to bypass or even contradict planetary influence should He wish. On the other hand, the fact that such divinatory astrology also restricts human free will is – for obvious reasons, given Calvin's theology – *not* a bone of contention, whereas it was for Pico.

Calvin's rhetoric, with its antithesis-based style (*elocutio*) and its lucid structure (*dispositio*), is intended to leave no room for doubt. But much vernacular writing on divination did leave such room. For example, Pontus de Tyard, whom we encountered earlier using the genre of dialogue to outline the neo-Platonic theory of frenzies, also used it to amplify the pros and cons of judicial astrology in his *Mantice: Discours de la verité de divination par astrologie* (1558). (Mantice, an interlocutor in the dialogue, is named after the Greek term for divination.) Tyard imitates Cicero in treating this topic in a dialogue form compatible with the philosophy of scepticism (**85**: pp.

15, 185). Although the dialogue culminates in a denunciation of judicial astrology (pp. 193-4), a vestige of doubt perhaps still lingers.

Doubt also accompanied condemnation when divination got onto the stage. For example, some 30 years before *Macbeth*, La Taille devoted the middle Act of his biblical tragedy *Saül le Furieux* to a spectacular staging of necromancy (divination by communication with the dead). While the play's main source is the Bible (1 Samuel 15-31), this scene also imitates Lucan's *Civil War* (*Pharsalia*, VI.675-739). Saül, the King of Israel, having disobeyed an order from God that the prophet Samuël had relayed to him, is now being punished by losing his war against the Philistines. Anxious to know what will happen if he fights on or gives up, Saül consults a necromancer: the Bible's Witch of Endor has here become a 'Phitonisse' (from the Greek for 'familiar spirit'). In an elaborate conjuration, laced with ceremonial black magic, she summons numerous bad demons, spirits and devils who compel (what seems to be) the reluctant spirit of the now dead Samuël to return. This spirit foretells Saül's downfall and his replacement by David. La Taille uses the chorus of Levites to make clear that Saül has compounded his initial sin of disobedience through the subsequent sin of necromancy. He serves as a cautionary example against divination.

However, whereas in Calvin's treatise – which also cites biblical and other examples among its proofs – such exemplarity is the whole point, here it is only part of the point. Both writers want to entertain. But La Taille wants to do so to an extent that flagrantly exceeds the stated moral purpose. By choosing to make the scene so sensational and thrilling, he gives audiences a rare chance to enjoy vicariously, with a clear conscience, what it would be reprehensible and dangerous for them to witness or instigate in real life.

Nonetheless, even for a dramatist, this is delicate ground on which to tread. So, in his preface, La Taille surrounds with doubt the question of exactly *what* is represented on stage. Is it really the spirit of Samuël? Or else some diabolic impersonation of it? Citing discrepant evidence on this point in the Bible, Cornelius Agrippa, and the ancient historian Flavius Josephus, La Taille remains non-committal, running for the cover of dramatic licence. A play is not a theological treatise (**56**: pp. 22-3).

Nor is a fictional chronicle. Rabelais's *Third Book* is a rich, doubt-laden exploration of divination. Panurge wants to get married but is anxious that his (as yet unchosen) wife might cuckold him. To discover if this will happen, he tries various methods of divination, including: Virgilian lots (interpreting a randomly selected line from Virgil); oneiromancy (interpreting a dream Panurge has had); and consultation with various people including a sibyl (prophetess), a deaf-mute, an old man nearing death, a magus and a madman.

Whereas the genre of the treatise lends itself to firm conclusions, Rabelais here uses a hybrid combination of genres – dominated by that of philosophical dialogue, to which Tyard also resorted – to explore the possibilities and dangers of divination. Certainly, some methods – Virgilian lots, oneiromancy, the deaf-mute, the dying old man, the madman – are represented as relatively respectable. How? By being proposed and (with one exception) witnessed by Panurge's serious-minded friend Pantagruel, who (sometimes) provides ancient and modern examples of their effectiveness, and (some-times) philosophical explanations of how they work. Justifying oneiromancy, for example, Pantagruel explains that when we are asleep our soul is temporarily freed from our body and

> reveoit sa patrie, qui est le ciel. De là receoit participation insigne de sa prime et divine origine, et en contemplation de ceste infinie et intellectuale sphaere, le centre de laquelle est en chascun lieu de l'univers, la circunference poinct (c'est Dieu scelon la doctrine de Hermes Trismegistus), à laquelle rien ne advient, rien ne passe, rien ne dechet, tous temps sont praesens: note non seulement les choses passées en mouvemens inferieurs, mais aussi les futures, et, les rapor-tant à son corps, et par les sens et organes d'icelluy les exposant aux amis, est dicte vaticinatrice et prophete. (**29**: p. 625)

again sees its native country, which is heaven. From there it receives notable participation in its primal rights, origin, and in contemplation of that infinite intellectual sphere whose centre is in every place and the circumference nowhere (that is God, according to the doctrine of Hermes Trismegistus), where nothing happens, nothing passes, nothing decays, [all times are present]; it notes not only things past in our movements here below but also future things; and, [communicating them to its body, and] by its senses and organs exposing them to friends, [the soul] is called soothsaying and prophetic. (**30**: p. 293)

In this neo-Platonic account, tinged with Hermetic ancient theology, when our soul is dreaming it contemplates a divine, purely intellectual, incorporeal 'sphere' or level of reality. To know this place of the cosmos, normally so remote, is also to know the future. But the divine message gets adulterated as it is transmitted down to our corporeal senses, which is why (as Pantagruel says after the passage quoted) oneiromancy is fallible. This philosophical explanation, like the others that Pantagruel offers, is also given gravitas by the Ciceronian hypotaxis.

On the other hand, judging by the same criteria, certain methods of divination are represented as more equivocal (the sibyl) or as less respectable – dice, oracles and prophets, the methods offered by the magus, omens. (The name of the magus, Her Trippa, partly alludes to Cornelius Agrippa.)

However, even among the apparently respectable methods, all are represented as potentially fallible, not just oneiromancy. As M.A. Screech has shown, Rabelais's portrayal of Panurge's search for absolute certainty evokes the view of some contemporaries that certain methods of divination are fine if they are used only as probable indicators, alongside other ways of making up one's mind about something, such as consulting one's own will (**49**: pp. 240-1). On the other hand, when Pantagruel and Panurge repeatedly produce conflicting interpretations of the mantic (divinatory) signs that the various methods produce (the deaf-mute's gestures, the line from Virgil and so on), it is not always clear that Pantagruel's interpretation is necessarily more plausible or self-evident than Panurge's. Rather, by devoting so much space to these interpreta-

tions, Rabelais seems to highlight the ingenious, creative and problematic nature of hermeneutics itself (the theory and practice of
interpretation), as we saw him doing in the *Fourth Book.*

Compared with Rabelais's equivocal treatment of divination,
Montaigne's later, shorter, but similarly wide-ranging survey of its
methods in the *Essais* ('Des pronostications', i.11) initially seems to
condemn it unequivocally. Even compared with Calvin (who still
accepts the principles of astrology) or La Taille (who represents
divination as undesirable rather than impossible), Montaigne seems
to deprive divination of any learned or metaphysical underpinning.
His arguments are partly rational (astrological predictions are sometimes correct by pure fluke), partly psychological (the *daimonion* or
personal demon which urged Socrates not to do certain things,
according to Plato and Plutarch, was in fact probably Socrates's own
will). Montaigne's arguments seem 'modern' in the sense of being
less strange to many twenty-first-century readers than others we
have encountered concerning divination. Indeed, when he notes
that many of the Greco-Roman methods of divination listed by
Cicero and others have been abolished by Christianity (p. 98), his
tone is closer to that of a detached anthropologist (noting this development), than to that of a theologian such as Calvin (advocating it).

However, we should be wary of projecting our own views back
onto Montaigne. It would be inaccurate to describe him as 'sceptical' about divination if by that we mean that he rejects it. Rather,
he is sceptical in the pyrrhonist sense of producing counter-argu-
ments against divination that culminate in a suspension of
judgement about it. (He treats witchcraft in a similar way in iii.11.)
Some classical passages (*loci*) are cited without it being clear what
the reader should make of them, such as Plato's proposal (*Republic,*
v.460) that sortition (the casting of lots) be used to arrange marriages
(p. 101). Moreover, even Montaigne's psychological interpretation
of Socrates' personal demon is tentative, hedged with a 'perhaps' ('à
l'aventure', p. 102). Indeed, when Montaigne then adds that he too
has experienced such non-rational promptings, he argues that the
success he had in obeying them suggests that 'elles pourraient être

jugées tenir quelque chose d'inspiration divine' ('they could have
been judged to contain something of divine inspiration'; p. 103; **12**:
p. 46). These words, the last in the chapter, point in an entirely
unexpected direction. Having extensively questioned whether we
can have an inkling of the future thanks to something that lies
outside us, Montaigne ends up *re-asserting* that possibility, albeit in
the characteristically minor key of the conditional tense. Like many
sixteenth-century discussions of divination, his combines doubt and
uncertainty with excitement and possibility.

6.4. Philosophical poetry

Divination was just one of many branches of natural and/or occult
philosophy that were transported into the vernacular in various
genres. One such genre, prominent in the second half of the
sixteenth century, was philosophical poetry. Ranging from a few
lines to thousands, philosophical poems described and imagined in
French the recesses of nature and of the cosmos. Their themes
included cosmology, astronomy, astrology, physics, metaphysics,
alchemy, soul, precious stones and meteorology (which was the
study of Earth's atmosphere, including – as for Aristotle – the
weather, meteors, comets, seas, rivers and mountains). The many
authors they imitated included ancient philosophical poets, especially Lucretius, but also Manilius, Aratus and Oppian. They also
reworked aspects of ancient epic poetry, as did D'Aubigné in his
long poem of a very different kind, *Les Tragiques*. In addition, some
imitated more recent neo-Latin poems – such as the hymns of the
fifteenth-century Greek humanist Michael Marullus (imitated by
Ronsard's hymns) or Buchanan's *Sphaera*, on astronomy (published
in 1585) – which were themselves imitations of ancient philosophical poetry.

This transfer of philosophy into French poetry disseminated
theories that some readers might not have encountered otherwise.
But the prime concern was not always pedagogical. It was often to
give poetic form to philosophy, to promote the newly prominent

notion that poetry was more apt than prose to convey truths about the cosmos. We have already encountered the aggrandizing, neo-Platonic views of poetic inspiration current among the Pléiade, which emphasized that much 'ancient theology' had been couched in allegory and poetry, for example in the hymns attributed to Orpheus, who was believed to have come next after Hermes Trismegistus in the chain of transmission. Ronsard's *Hymnes* (1555 and 1556) are partly modelled on this imagined tradition. They include cosmological and occult philosophy (as well as moral themes and panegyric or praise). For instance, 'Les Daimons' is a dazzling description – based on neo-Platonic sources – of good and bad demons and the places they frequent. Creatures of the air, 'habitans les confins / De la terre et du ciel' ('inhabiting the confines of earth and heaven'), these intermediate beings, between God and humans, commute down to Earth to torment us or to tell us God's will (**31**: i, p. 489; **32**: p. 149).

But a radical difference between French and ancient philosophical poetry was the former's Christianity, sometimes discreet, sometimes emphatic. Like authors of French biblical tragedy, some philosophical poets superimposed imitation of the Bible on their imitation of ancients, in this case the heretical, materialist Lucretius and others. These French poets, taking their cue from the Book of Genesis and from commentaries on it such as the *Hexaemeron* by the Church Father St Ambrose, composed long 'hexaemeral' poems, that is, ones structured by the six days of Creation (followed by the seventh, on which God rested). For example, Scève's *Microcosme* was published in 1562, long after his love poetry.

6.4.1. Guillaume de Saluste Du Bartas, 'La Sepmaine'

Then, in 1578, there appeared the most commercially successful – and perhaps the greatest – French philosophical poem of all, the hexaemeral *La Sepmaine* (*The Week*) by Guillaume de Saluste Du Bartas.

Over 6,000 lines long, divided into seven days, it is a vast amplification of the opening of Genesis (1-2:2). Du Bartas describes firstly matter, light, angels (Day 1), then the four elements, the realm of the air, the structure of the cosmos (Day 2), then the realms of water (rivers and so on) and of the Earth (mines, rustic life, and so on) (Day 3), then the stars, planets, celestial spheres (Day 4), then fish and birds (Day 5), then animals, man, woman (Day 6), and finally God's providence and the world's order (Day 7). Du Bartas planned a follow-up, a 'second week', vaster still, several times longer than the first. It began appearing in 1584, as *La Seconde Sepmaine*, but less than half was completed. It was to be a history of humanity from Eden to the Last Judgement.

La Sepmaine is an extraordinary projection of swathes of ancient learning (mediated by humanism) onto the hexaemeral framework provided by Genesis. The aim is to provide a philosophical description of the world that is not dry, systematic and entirely coherent but that inspires wonder (*admiration*) at God's handiwork. Du Bartas was a Calvinist. The poem's hexaemeral structure is intended to show that God's revelation of Himself in the Bible squares with what can be found in God's other great book, nature itself (Day 1, ll. 151-78). (This Book of Nature metaphor was commonplace.) In Du Bartas's perspective, poetry is better placed than prose to inspire wonder. His poetry milks the resources of rhetoric. Its *elocutio* is dazzling, rich, 'copious', extravagant, full of metaphor, simile, hyperbole, circumlocution, neologism, and so on. Literary critics used to call this kind of style 'Baroque'. D'Aubigné uses it mainly for shock, but his contemporary Du Bartas mainly for awe. They show that not all Calvinists promoted aesthetic ideals of sobriety and simplicity.

On the other hand, *La Sepmaine* was pedagogical as well as devotional. In the form in which most people read it, it offered considerable instruction, including some on the hidden recesses of nature and cosmos. The poem was most often printed together with an extensive running commentary in prose by fellow Calvinist Simon Goulart, which grew out of Goulart's annotations to the 1581 edition. A rival Catholic commentary, by Pantaléon Thévenin, was also produced (1585) – the poem's success transcended religious divisions. Whereas it was common practice for ancient texts to be accompanied by modern commentaries, it was unprecedented for a modern French poem to be given this treatment (with the exception of Ronsard's learning-laden *Amours*, on which Muret and Rémy Belleau published commentaries in 1553 and 1560). This gave the modern poem authoritative, quasi-ancient status. Goulart's commentary is a lucid, systematic introduction to the philosophy that Du Bartas covers more spectacularly and demandingly. So the poems' early editions represented the world to readers in two ways: through humdrum explanatory prose and poetical pyrotechnics. This compromise was the latest twist in the controversial relationship between philosophy and rhetoric, about which we earlier saw humanists and scholastics disagree.

Despite its pedagogical dimension, *La Sepmaine* is not didactic in the sense of claiming to be always right. Especially when Du Bartas enters the more speculative realms of philosophy, investigating the recesses of nature and cosmos, he expresses the kind of uncertainty that we encountered in some vernacular treatment of divination. For example, what is the celestial realm above the moon made of?

> Mais de quelle matiere, ô Maistre ingenieux,   887
> Formeray-je apres toy les courbeures des Cieux? [...]
>
> Par le docte Lycee ores je me promene: 893
> Ore l'Academie en ses ombres me mene.
> Mes pas dessus les pas d'Aristote imprimant
> Je prive d'elemens le doré firmament.
> J'en banni tout meslange, et croy que la puissance
> De Dieu l'a façonné d'une cinquiesme essence [...]
>
> Puis soudain revenant disciple studieux   919
> De l'Attique Platon je les mets dans les cieux. [...]
>
> Non que je face esgaux les corps dont je compose   929
> Ce corps, qui de son rond embrasse toute chose,
> A ces lourds elemens, qu'ici bas les humains

Et voyent de leurs yeux, et touchent de leurs mains.
Ils sont tous beaux, tous purs, une saincte harmonie
D'un eternel lien tient leur substance unie [...]

Voila jusqu'où s'estend la superbe fureur   939
Des hommes aveuglez d'ignorance et d'erreur,
Qui, comme s'ils avoyent mile fois calcinee
La matiere d'enhaut, d'une langue effrenee,
Osent ascertener, sans preuve et sans raison,
De quel bois l'Eternel charpenta sa maison.
Or cent fois j'aime mieux demeurer en ce doute,   945
Qu'en errant faire errer le simple qui m'escoute,
Attendant qu'un saint Paul redescende des cieux:
Ou bien, que deschargé du manteau vicieux
De ce rebelle corps, qui mon ame sans cesse
D'un pesant contrepoids en bas presse et represse,   950
Moy-mesme j'aille voir les beautez de ce lieu:
Si lors je veux rien voir que la face de Dieu. (Day 2)

But, following you, skilled Master, out of what shall I make the
heavenly spheres? [...] First I walk through the learned Lyceum;
then the Academy leads me into its shades. Following in Aristotle's
footsteps, I deprive the golden firmament of elements. I banish all
mixture from it, and believe that God's power fashioned it out of a
fifth essence. [...] Then, suddenly turning back into a conscientious
student of Attic Plato, I put the elements in the heavens. [...] Not
that I make those bodies, those elements – out of which I assemble
the body which holds everything within its circular embrace –
identical to those heavy elements which humans, down here
below, both see with their eyes and touch with their hands. The
ones in the heavens are entirely beautiful and pure; their substance
is held together by the eternal bond of a holy harmony. [...] See
how far arrogant madness leads men who are blinded by ignorance and error and who, without proof or reason, dare to assert
dogmatically what wood the Eternal crafted his house out of, as if
they had reduced to dust on countless occasions the matter that's

up there. I, on the other hand, much prefer to remain uncertain about this issue rather than making any uneducated reader of mine err through my own error. I prefer to wait until St Paul returns from heaven or until I myself – when unburdened of this unruly body's vicious mantle, which continually drags down my soul, again and again, with its weighty counter-weight – go to see that beautiful place. And yet I'll then want to see nothing but the face of God.

Going beyond what we *can* see and touch (two external senses privileged by the syntactic parallelism between the hemistichs of line 932), Du Bartas first speculates that Aristotle was right to claim that the heavens are made of quintessence, aether. But the poet then conjectures that there is no such thing as this perfect fifth element, and that instead Plato was right to argue that the heavens (designated by circumlocution in line 930) are composed of a stable mixture of the familiar four elements, which are always mixed unstably in our sub-lunar world. Although Plato's theory establishes a distinction between the imperfect sensible realm and the perfect intelligible one, it postulates more intimate connections between the two realms – including between microcosm and macrocosm – than does Aristotle's, by supposing that both are made of the same matter.

Who is right? The poet's hesitation here expresses the unsettling impact of humanism on 'science'. Scholasticism's status as a widely accepted explanatory framework has now been challenged by a multiplicity of ancient '-isms', of which Platonism is just one. All have their attractions, but none replaces scholasticism as a new source of consensus about even basic tenets, such as what the heavens are made of. What should one believe given that ancient authorities disagree among themselves? The poet represents his search for certainty as a walk through Aristotle's school (Lyceum) and Plato's Academy, which is set among the 'shades' (l. 894) of olive groves (recalling the shadows that, for Plato, are all we can see of true reality). Du Bartas here provides another version of the humanist-inspired, present tense, day-dreaming time travel that we saw Machiavelli describe. Yet the walk through history is not chronological. Although Aristotle was Plato's pupil, the poet visits Aristotle first, because scholasticism had long made his opinion the standard one ('la commune opinion', comments Goulart at this point) (**86**: i, p. 81 n.).

The poet concludes by refusing to conclude in human terms. He shifts attention from the other times and places of antiquity to the future in which he – like D'Aubigné's persona at the end of *Les Tragiques* – will be transported to the far 'place' (l. 951) of the cosmos and to God's other world. The Bible trumps pagan antiquity: Du Bartas alludes indirectly to St Paul's famous desire for death (l. 957; Philippians 1:23). But even the anticipated liberation is described in neo-Platonic terms (ll. 949-50): the body's downward pressure on the pining soul is imitated by the deliberately heavy-handed 'presse et represse' – this *polyptoton* creates rich, stodgy rhyme within the line. With Christianized scepticism, the poet suspends judgement for the time being. *La Sepmaine* is not a thoroughgoing pyrrhonist work. Indeed, it claims to tell many truths about the world. But on several points it also refrains from adjudicating between competing theories. The epistemological triad has fallen short: neither authority (the ancients), nor experience (hands-on evidence of the senses, ll. 941-2), nor reason (l. 943) can decide what the heavens are made of.

However, the process of *trying* to decide produces wonder – not just at the cosmic handiwork that eludes our grasp, but also at our imaginative efforts to grasp it. Human ingenuity, although incapable of fully knowing the created world, and although arrogant if it forgets this, is itself one part of that world. Its powers are imperfect, but amazing. Thus, the poet casts himself here not just as a would-be recorder of the real, but as a sub-creator in his own right. From the opening apostrophe to God (l. 887) onwards, the poet describes *himself* as creating various possible worlds through the very act of describing them. The lines I have had to omit from the passage vividly amplify what the heavens *would* be like if composed of aether or else of a perfect mixture of elements. *La Sepmaine*, with its fertile, 'copious' imaginings of what is, of what may be, or even of what is not (for example Day 4, ll. 125-60), is presented as being itself part of the rich Creation that it celebrates.

Selected reading

Texts

83. Jean Calvin, *Advertissement contre l'astrologie judiciaire*, ed. O. Millet (Geneva, 1985).

84. François Rabelais, *Pantagrueline prognostication pour l'an 1533*, ed. M.A. Screech (Geneva, 1974). A spoof astrological almanac. This edition also includes serious almanacs by Rabelais and others.

85. Pontus de Tyard, *Mantice: Discours de la verité de divination par astrologie*, ed. S. Bokdam (Geneva, 1990).

Philosophical poetry

86. Guillaume de Saluste Du Bartas, *La Sepmaine*, ed. Y. Bellenger, 2 vols (Paris, 1981). Extracts from Goulart's commentary are quoted in the footnotes.

Studies

See also **5**, which outlines the connections between philosophy, science, and humanism, and **6**, of which Section VI is on natural philosophy, astrology, and magic, and Section IX on psychology and soul.

87. A. Debus, *Man and Nature in the Renaissance* (Cambridge, 1978). Introduction to scientific thought.

88. S. Shapin, *The Scientific Revolution* (Chicago and London, 1996). Introduction to the most innovative strands of sixteenth- and seventeenth-century scientific thought.

89. N. Siraisi, *Medieval and Early Renaissance Medicine: An Introduction to Knowledge and Practice* (Chicago and London, 1990).

90. J. Tester, *A History of Western Astrology* (Woodbridge, 1987).

Philosophical poetry

91. Y. Bellenger, *Du Bartas et ses divines Semaines* (Paris, 1993).

92. P. Ford, *Ronsard's 'Hymnes': A Literary and Iconographical Study* (Tempe, 1997).

'Our world has just discovered another one': Clashing Continents

The remote places imagined also included continents beyond Europe. The existence of Asia and Africa had long been known. But the Americas were new – not to the 70-80 million who probably inhabited them in 1500, but to the Europeans because of whose presence, violence and germs that population fell to about 10 million by 1550.

The enormity of Europe's impact on the Americas was not yet reciprocated in the sixteenth century, when this fourth continent's official 'discovery' – inaugurated in the 1490s by Christopher Columbus (an Italian working for Ferdinand and Isabella of Spain) – had no material impact on most Europeans' lives. But it did already have an impact on many imaginations (especially those of the literate), thanks to the new medium of print. Like the recesses of nature and cosmos, the Americas were widely imagined through frameworks provided by classical and biblical antiquity. Remote times about which much seemed to be known were thus projected onto a contemporary place about which little was known.

7.1. 'Our world ...': Frenchness in flux

Imagining other continents mostly bolstered rather than unsettled people's sense of what Montaigne, in my title quotation, calls 'our world'. The boundaries of most educated French people's 'world' were defined by, for example, their land (if they were noble), their region, their most prominent vernacular (French, with which the

1539 Ordonnance of Villers-Cotterêts replaced Latin as the official language of legal documents), their monarchy, their belonging to the French polity or commonwealth (*res publica* in Latin, *république* in French), to Christendom itself, and to 'Europe' (a concept derived from ancient myth and popularized by humanism). For 'our world' to be superior, it needed another 'world' to be superior *to* – in religion, culture, technology – and the three other continents were imagined to duly oblige.

However, the boundaries of 'our world' were hardly stable. Even on a physical level, France fluctuated, for example with the annexation of several territories in the late fifteenth century (Burgundy, Anjou, Maine, Provence and Brittany). It therefore seemed more apt to define 'France' by its history than by its frontiers. But how exactly? This was much disputed. Chronicles composed in the Middle Ages had often argued that France had been founded by the Franks, one of whom, Pharamond, in the early fifth century, was the first king. The Franks then became Christian with the conversion of Clovis (late fifth century), who founded the Merovingian dynasty, later followed by the Carolingian and Capetian ones. Such chronicles had often claimed that the Franks were actually descended from a group of Trojans who, centuries earlier, under their leader Francio, had fled from the ancient Greek sack of Troy.

In the sixteenth century, some still presented the French as Trojans. This connected the modern monarchy and people to venerable antiquity. Ronsard's unfinished *Franciade* (1572) was a dynastic epic poem modelled on Virgil's *Aeneid*. As Virgil locates the origins of Rome in one Trojan refugee (Aeneas), so Ronsard locates those of the French monarchy in another (Francion, whom Ronsard identifies as Astyanax, son of the Trojan hero Hector). Yet Ronsard does not claim that this genealogy is historically true. He describes himself as writing what could have happened (poetry), rather than what did (history) (**31**: i, pp. 1167-8).

Even this Trojan story fluctuated, depending on the image of France required. The common origins of Aeneas and Francio implied that the French had blood ties to the Romans and so to modern Italians and popes. This hardly appealed to French Gallicans and Protestants. So the Italian connection was downplayed by the Gallican Lemaire de Belges, in his prose work *Les Illustrations de Gaule et Singularités de Troie* (1510-13). He introduced the ingenious argument that the Trojans were themselves descended from ... the Gauls! So when Francus or Francio settled in what is now France he was in a sense coming home.

Some humanist historiographers increasingly rejected the Trojan genealogy as untrue. But they did focus on ancient Gaul that, largely ignored by earlier, medieval chronicles, now seemed crucial to defining France through its history. Lawyers in particular, ranging from the Gallican Catholic Étienne Pasquier to the Calvinist François Hotman, emphasized the continuity between ancient Gaul and modern France. Their more scholarly, critical use of sources made them, in some ways, the precursors of today's would-be objective historians. Yet their purpose in making certain images of Gaul normative for the present was to intervene politically in that present: France should have its own distinct customs and laws, a ruler whose power is limited by French institutions, and little or no connection with Rome.

Such disputes about the nature of 'our world' show in themselves that that world was fractured, not least by religious schism. Christendom, already divided between West and East, was now further subdivided in the West by the Reformation. To make matters worse, the argument that Europe belonged almost entirely to Christendom now seemed less plausible because of the Ottoman Empire's expansion. Following the fall of Constantinople (1453) and other Ottoman Turk victories, their 1529 siege of Vienna (despite failing) reinforced the impression that Islam had once again infiltrated Europe, this time from Asia, so soon after the 1492 expulsion of Muslims (and Jews) from Spain: 'du costé de la mer nous avons ces barbares pres de nos portes, & du costé de la terre, nous les avons dedans nos portes' ('out at sea the barbarians are close to our gates, and inland they are within them'; **94**: p. 439), as François de La Noue put it (1587).

French writers ranging from the Protestant leader and soldier La Noue to the anti-Protestant diplomat René de Lucinge called for new, anti-Ottoman crusades. Alongside these writers' claims of Christian superiority over the supposedly cruel, barbaric, treacherous and impious 'Turks' can be detected anxieties of inferiority, especially regarding the Ottomans' military success, organization and high standards of material well-being. This troubling dimension of the 'Turks' was enhanced by the fact that they had divided Christendom: La Noue condemns the 1535 Franco-Ottoman alliance agreed by François Ier (against the Habsburg Holy Roman Emperor, Charles V) as the latest of many shameful Christian pacts with this infidel (p. 427). On the other hand, La Noue's peroration suggests that this threatening Other can be used to heal the fractures of 'Our world': by uniting against the 'Turk', Catholics and Protestants can remind themselves that they are brothers in Christ (pp. 515-16).

7.2. '... another one'? The Americas

Compared with the 'Turks', Amerindians seemed readier grist to the mill of European superiority. Nonetheless, so disorienting was the news from this 'New World' that a few Europeans even questioned that superiority.

Large-scale French expeditions to the Americas were rare in the sixteenth century. Moreover, only in 1608, with Samuel de Champlain's Québec, was the first lasting French settlement there founded. Decades earlier, François Ier hoped to join in the ongoing Iberian carve-up of the Americas. He focused on what is now Canada, having persuaded Pope Clement VIII to concede that the 1493 'Papal Donation' of the 'New World' to Spain and Portugal applied only to lands already effectively occupied. There were three French royal-backed expeditions (1534-43) to what soon became known as Canada. The master mariner Jacques Cartier led the first two and participated in the third, which was officially led by a nobleman, Roberval. Cartier eventually sailed up the St Lawrence river to Stadacona (the site of present-day Québec City) and Hochelaga (now Montreal). He encountered, and had increasingly hostile relations with, Iroquoian-speaking people, especially the Stadaconans. The voyages' evolving aims included discovering the fabled north-west passage to the Orient, plundering mines of precious minerals and metals, fostering the fur trade that began to develop, and, in the third expedition, establishing a settlement.

The Canada venture failed. French attention turned to more clement climes, first Brazil. In 1555, an expedition led by Nicolas Durand de Villegagnon took control of the bay of Guanabara (Rio de Janeiro) and allied itself with one of the local Indian tribes, the Tupinambá. However, the fortress Villegagnon built there was overrun by the Portuguese in 1560. The expedition's main aim seems to have been to further French commercial interests. Although backed by Henri II, it may also have been for some a first step towards a possible Huguenot refuge from persecution at home. That aim, as well as that of unnerving Spanish settlements in the Caribbean, may also have informed the next venture, a Huguenot-dominated one to Florida (1564-65), with unofficial support from Charles IX, which ended in notorious massacres by Spanish forces of most of the would-be French settlers.

These encounters, although brief, long resonated in the memories and imaginations of those who wrote and read about them. Paradoxically, as the century progressed and major French expeditions ceased (with the Wars of Religion providing other priorities), disquiet provoked by Amerindian otherness bubbled more to the surface.

Already in Cartier's lifetime, in 1545, a first-hand account of one of his Canadian voyages (the second) was published. It had not been intended primarily for publication, but by now, with the venture's failure, there was no point in secrecy. The accounts of the other two voyages were only published later, in foreign translations. The accounts refer to Cartier in the third person but were probably wholly or partly composed by him. They are ship journals and reports to François Ier on topography and natural resources. Their aim is not the objectivity to which an ethnographic study of today might aspire. Rather, they outline and facilitate the prospects for future French expeditions, whether by charting bays and bird life or claiming that this people would be readily subjugated ('aisé à dompter') and easily converted to our holy faith ('facille [...] à convertir à notre saincte foy'; **96**: pp. 162, 113). The intention is also to justify Cartier's decisions, which are presented as being based on a firm understanding of the Indians' minds, as expressed through their word, deed and gesture, such as supposed signs of joy ('signes de joye', p. 115).

However, numerous blind spots, gaps, silences, contradictions in the representation of the Indians suggest that this hermeneutic confidence is misplaced. For example, these 'savages' seem easy to convert, are allegedly impressed by Cartier's praying (p. 155), are apparently delighted when their own deities' predictions of imminent French deaths from the cold are contradicted by Christ's own predictions (p. 145), and yet they persist with their own gods. As Bruce Trigger has shown, this behaviour can perhaps be explained by the Iroquoian assumption that it is improper and impolite to question other people's beliefs (**107**: i, p. 190). Indeed, although we can suspect such misunderstandings if we read the French accounts against the grain, the suspicions are deepened (without becoming certainties) by the research of a historical anthropologist such as Trigger, with his knowledge of Iroquoian culture, which was oral, not written. For instance, Trigger suggests that Cartier repeatedly misunderstands the reasons for the Stadaconans' attempts to dissuade him from venturing further up the St Lawrence to visit Hochelaga. Cartier surmises, probably wrongly, that the Stadaconans were subjects of the Hochelagans (**96**: p. 153; **107**: i, p. 180). He interprets as bribes, tricks and threats what were probably various Stadaconan attempts to establish an alliance guaranteeing them the position of middleman in the trading of European goods with the interior – the first of many such attempts made in the region over the decades to come (**96**: pp. 140-6: **107**, i, pp. 187-8).

Thus, if Cartier's reports gesture towards Amerindian otherness, towards something that exceeds their own grasp, it is despite themselves. The same is broadly true of much writing about other continents, such as that of André Thevet, who was decisive in establishing the newly prestigious discipline of geography or 'cosmography' – description of everywhere on Earth. Thevet shared Cartier's hermeneutic confidence. Like Cartier, he was not from the gentry and so had no humanist education. But, unlike Cartier, he superimposed an ancient grid on the places, peoples and animals he wrote about. He did this by employing humanist-trained assistants (Mathurin Héret and François de Belleforest) to lace his text with references to Pliny the Elder, Herodotus, Diodorus Siculus, Strabo and others, establishing parallels or contrasts between Thevet's and the ancients' first- or second-hand alleged observations of exotica ('singularités').

One of Thevet's works (*Les Singularités de la France Antarctique,* 1557) is presented as a description of the voyage to Brazil and back (1555-56) that Thevet had just completed, having gone with Villegagnon. In contrast to Cartier, Thevet saw very little of what he describes. He was bedridden for much of his own short stay in Guanabara. However, even when he openly acknowledges that he includes observations made by others, such as Cartier in Canada (**99**: p. 278), Thevet emphasizes that he did at least sail relatively *close* to North America and stuck his head out of the ship in its direction (p. 273). So he strains to its limits the autopsy (first-person eyewitnessing) that guaranteed cosmography's truthfulness (and that corresponded to 'experience' in the epistemological triad of authority-reason-experience).

By contrast, Jean de Léry, in his later account of the same Brazil expedition, promoted autopsy in a stricter, narrower sense, thereby gesturing more towards Amerindian otherness. Léry was one of the Calvinists who reinforced the expedition in 1557, before a dispute with Villegagnon over the Eucharist resulted in some of them, including Léry, sailing back to France in dire conditions in 1558. The aims of Léry's *Histoire d'un voyage faict en la terre du Bresil* (1578) include justifying the Calvinists' behaviour and condemning

Villegagnon's. Blaming Villegagnon for the downfall of the settlement known as 'Antarctic France', Léry mourns a lost opportunity
rather than providing, like Thevet and Cartier, a prospectus for
future colonial expeditions. Léry condemns the enemy-eating
Tupinambá as hell-bound 'savages' abandoned by God. They are
perhaps descended from Ham (Cham), who was cursed by his
father Noah (p. 421; Genesis 9:20-5). (Europeans were believed to
be descendants of another of Noah's sons, Japhet.) Léry thus superimposes biblical antiquity on the Tupinambá, having been relatively
restrained from superimposing the Greco-Roman past, of which he
too, a cobbler turned preacher, had little humanist knowledge.

That relative restraint reinforces Léry's claim to describe only what
he saw, unlike the Catholic liar Thevet (pp. 98, 105-6). Although even
Léry's claim is probably exaggerated, his commitment to strict
autopsy makes him write chorography or topography (description of
one place) rather than cosmography. By claiming only to view from a
particular angle, Léry gains credibility and yet loses the need to cover
all angles, to claim to understand everything about the Tupinambá.
Thus, despite the eschatology (theology concerning the end of the
world) with which he damns them, he wonders whether it might have
been possible to convert some of them after all (p. 414). Even his Ham
genealogy is only presented as a conjecture. He accepts that his book,
for all its recourse to the rhetorical figure of *enargia* (vivid description,
for example, pp. 226-7), and even with its engravings, fails to repro-
duce the more accurate picture of the Indians that sits in his
imagination (pp. 233-4). He acknowledges that he fails to understand
some Indian practices, particularly various 'choses doublement
estranges et vrayement esmerveillables' ('things doubly strange and
truly amazing') involving women, such as their preference for nudity
(p. 231). As Stephen Greenblatt has shown, in European writing
about the 'New World' such vocabulary of wonder is often the
symptom of an impasse of understanding. Usually in the period, the
impasse does not cause any slow-down of the drive towards literal or
conceptual possession of the marvels described. But in a few writers
it does: one is Léry, another Montaigne (**104**).

The two main discussions of the 'New World' in Montaigne's *Essais* are 'Des cannibales' (i.30) and 'Des coches' ('On coaches', iii.6). The first focuses on the Tupinambá, the second on the Spanish destruction of the civilizations of the Aztecs in Mexico and the Incas in Peru. Montaigne argues that Europeans are inferior in some respects. Tupinambá cannibalism is perhaps barbaric, but less so than the roasting and feeding to animals of live bodies that occurred in the Wars of Religion (11: p. 325). It is our unscrupulousness, our moral inferiority to the Aztecs and Incas that has enabled us to defeat them (p. 1424). This first-person plural extends the guilt from the *conquistadores* to all Europeans and so radicalizes the more specific point scoring of the Calvinist Léry, who favourably compares cannibal honesty to the deceitfulness of Italian Catholics (Catherine de' Medici and her entourage) who control France (98: p. 508). (Montaigne read Léry shortly before writing 'Des cannibales'.)

However, using Amerindians to criticize Europe is different from seeking to represent them in anything like their own terms. Montaigne's knowledge of Amerindians was limited mainly to Spanish and French sources he used (without acknowledgement) and to his alleged conversations with a servant of his (who had lived in Brazil) and with three Tupinambá whom Montaigne encountered in Rouen in 1562 (11: pp. 317, 332). The negative mode which opens his description of the Tupinambá – they have no trade, no learning, no political hierarchy – makes them ciphers, utopian inversions of 'our world' (p. 320). Classical antiquity shapes Montaigne's Amerindians more profoundly than Léry's or even Thevet's. For example, the eloquence and heroic virtue of the last Aztec emperor (Cuauhtémoc) and of the Inca king (Atahualpa), executed in 1521 and 1533 respectively, match any found in antiquity (p. 1424). Moreover, despite Montaigne's denunciation of the *conquista*, his classicizing framework still idealizes colonial conquests, although only ones that might have been: had Alexander the Great or the Greeks and Romans conquered American peoples then they would have improved rather than destroyed them (pp. 1425-6).

The unprecedented relativism of Montaigne's discussions of the 'New World' proved extremely influential in centuries to come. It questions, and focuses to an unusual degree on, the relation *between* 'our world' and 'another one'. Yet, paradoxically, Montaigne is so preoccupied with problematizing the European perspective that in some ways he provides even fewer glimpses of the elusive otherness of Amerindian culture than do the more obviously Eurocentric texts of the travellers Cartier, Thevet and Léry, who all include far more details, including of Amerindian languages. Although Montaigne praises Cuauhtémoc, Atahualpa and the Tupinambá, he does not even mention their names.

Selected reading

Texts

93. Étienne Pasquier, *Les Recherches de la France*, 3 vols, ed. M.-M. Fragonard and F. Roudaut (Paris, 1996). Pasquier's history of France.

On 'Turks'

94. François de La Noue, *Discours politiques et militaires*, ed. F. Sutcliffe (Geneva, 1967), Chapters 21-2.
95. René de Lucinge, *De la naissance, durée et chute des estats*, ed. M. Heath (Geneva, 1984).

The Americas

96. Jacques Cartier, *Relations*, ed. M. Bideaux (Montreal, 1986). First-hand accounts of Cartier's expeditions.
97. ———, *The Voyages*, tr. H. Biggar (Toronto, Buffalo, London, 1993).
98. Jean de Léry, *Histoire d'un voyage en terre de Brésil*, ed. F. Lestringant (Paris, 1994).
99. André Thevet, *Le Brésil d'André Thevet: Les Singularités de la France Antarctique (1557)*, ed. F. Lestringant (Paris, 1997).

Studies

100. M. Heath, *Crusading Commonplaces: La Noue, Lucinge and Rhetoric against the Turks* (Geneva, 1986).

101. T. Hampton, *Literature and Nation in the Sixteenth Century: Inventing Renaissance France* (New York, 2001). Advanced. On the construction of 'France' in Rabelais, M. de Navarre, Du Bellay, Montaigne and others.

102. G. Huppert, *The Idea of Perfect History: Historical Erudition and Historical Philosophy in Renaissance France* (Urbana and Chicago, 1970). Chapters 3 and 4 are on humanist attempts to define 'France' through historiography.

103. F. Lestringant, *Mapping the Renaissance World: The Geographical Imagination in the Age of Discovery*, tr. D. Fausett (Berkeley, 1994). On Thevet's cosmography. Includes a chapter on Brazil.

The Americas

104. S. Greenblatt, *Marvelous Possessions: The Wonder of the New World* (Chicago, 1991). On Montaigne, Léry and many others.

105. F. Lestringant, *Cannibals: The Discovery and Representation of the Cannibal from Columbus to Jules Verne*, tr. R. Morris (Cambridge, 1997). Includes discussion of Léry and Montaigne.

106. B. Marshall (ed.), *France and the Americas: Culture, Politics, and History*, 3 vols (Santa Barbara, Denver, Oxford, 2005). An encyclopaedia. See entries for Brazil, Cartier, Champlain, Florida, François Ier, Montaigne and Roberval.

107. B. Trigger, *The Children of Aataentsic I: A History of the Huron People to 1660*, 2 vols (Montreal and London, 1976). Chapter 4 tries to reconstruct from the Iroquoians' perspective their encounters with Cartier's expeditions.

8

Conclusion: Lost Worlds?

Educated sixteenth-century imaginations were filled with overlapping worlds, with times and places located in the past and the future, within nature and beyond it. The usual point of those imaginings was the better to live life in the present. But they have now become, in their turn, worlds remote from us, known to us only partially, just as antiquity or the 'New World' were to them.

Many people sought to stave off the future loss of knowledge about their own present: we saw Budé advising François Ier to get his deeds written up by eloquent chroniclers. But some predicted huge losses. An unsettling parody of humanist learning, *Le Moyen de parvenir* (*The Way to Succeed, c.* 1616) by François Béroalde de Verville, is a mock banquet involving some 400 mostly famous people from all periods. It begins by evoking, in the style of a humanist historian, the recent switch from hard to soft balls in the *jeu de paume* (a precursor of tennis), predicting that it will throw future historians into confusion about the period as a whole (i, p. 33). In a more serious register, Montaigne's 'On coaches' evokes the destruction of Amerindian civilizations in order to show how knowledge of basic features of past cultures – such as the palls on which Aztecs carried their kings – constantly evaporates.

Many of the gaps in our own knowledge of sixteenth-century literature and thought are factual. For example, was Louise Labé actually a courtisan in whose name a group of men wrote poetry? This hypothesis, recently advanced by Mireille Huchon, seems improbable but is difficult to prove or disprove (**109**). If accepted, it would require the poetry to be read differently. But the poetry would still be remarkable. Even in cases where underlying facts are certain, textual interpretations are not. Indeed, those advanced in the present book could be contested. Our understanding of sixteenth-century writing depends on the method adopted, as John O'Brien has shown (**110**: pp. 1-52).

On the other hand, as humanism showed, one *can* retrieve lost fragments of the past (although their significance is altered in the process). Indeed, the humanist project of reanimating antiquity, while no longer culturally central today, still continues in some respects – witness the recent discovery of some texts by the ancient Greek mathematician Archimedes, concealed since the thirteenth century. What we can be certain of is that our own future will bring further gains, as well as losses, in our understanding of the largely submerged world of sixteenth-century literature and thought.

Selected reading

Texts

108. François Béroalde de Verville, *Le Moyen de parvenir*, 2 vols, ed. H. Moreau, A. Tournon, and J.-L. Ristori (Paris, 2004).

Studies

109. M. Huchon, *Louise Labé, une créature de papier* (Geneva, 2006). Controversial denial of Labé's authorship.

110. J. O'Brien and M. Quainton (eds), *Distant Voices Still Heard: Contemporary Readings of French Renaissance Literature* (Liverpool, 2000). O'Brien's Introduction surveys critical and theoretical approaches.

Glossary of Writers and Texts

Note: Most wrote some or all of their works in French, but some, especially humanist scholars, wrote only in Latin.

Alciato, Andrea (1492-1550): Italian humanist jurist; taught influentially in France; wrote a hugely successful book of emblems (moral poems accompanied by engravings).

Amadis de Gaule: enormously popular chivalric romance, adapted into French from 1540 onwards.

Amboise, Catherine d' (1482-1550): wrote various works (unprinted), including devotional poetry.

Amyot, Jacques (1513-93): translated Greek works (including Plutarch) into French.

Aneau, Barthélemy (?-1561): wrote fiction, history and a treatise on poetics.

Baïf, Jean-Antoine de (1532-89): Pléiade poet; son of Lazare.

Baïf, Lazare (*c.* 1496-1547): humanist and diplomat.

Belleau, Remy (1528-77): Pléiade poet and dramatist.

Belleforest, François de (1530-83): writer, adapter and compiler.

Belon, Pierre (*c.* 1517-65): naturalist and traveller.

Bertaut, Jean (1552-1611): poet.

Bèze, Théodore de (1519-1605): Calvinist leader, theologian and writer.

Billon, François de (*c.* 1522-*c.* 1566): wrote a pro-women treatise.

Boaistuau, Pierre (?-1566): adapted *Wondrous stories* (*Histoires prodigieuses*) from Italian into French.

Bodin, Jean (1520-96): influential political philosopher.

Bouchet, Guillaume (*c.* 1513-93): wrote a miscellany of post-prandial bourgeois conversations (*Serées*).

Bouchet, Jean (1467-*c.* 1557-59): historian, *rhétoriqueur* poet.

Bourbon, Gabrielle de (?-1516): religious writer.

Bourbon, Nicolas (1503-*c.* 1549): neo-Latin poet.

Bouvelles, Charles de (*c.* 1480-1533): philosopher and theologian, influenced by neo-Platonism.

Brantôme, Pierre de Bourdeille de (*c.* 1540-1614): wrote gossipy, salacious memoirs, printed posthumously.

Briçonnet, Guillaume (1472-1534): reforming bishop.

Briet de Crenne, Marguerite (*c.* 1510-*c.* 1552): as 'Helisenne de Crenne', she published fiction, an allegory and letters.

Bruès, Guy de: wrote a dialogue (1557) on scepticism.

Buchanan, George (1506-82): Scottish humanist; taught in France; wrote neo-Latin poetry and drama.

Budé, Guillaume (1468-1540): the greatest French humanist.

Bugnyon, Philibert (*c.* 1530-87): humanist, jurist and poet.

Buttet, Marc-Claude de (*c.* 1530-86): poet.

Calvin, Jean (1509-64): theologian; foremost leader of the French Reformation.

Canaye, Philippe (1551-1610): adapted Aristotle's writings on logic into French.

Cartier, Jacques (1491-1557): made three voyages to Canada; first-hand accounts survive.

Casaubon, Isaac (1559-1614): leading humanist; Protestant.

Champier, Symphorien (1471-1537/39): humanist, physician and polymath.

Chandieu, Antoine de Laroche (1534-91): Protestant theologian and poet.

Chappuys, Gabriel (1546?-*c.* 1613): translated many key Italian and Spanish works into French.

Charron, Pierre (1541-1603): cleric whose famous treatise on wisdom systematized and distorted Montaigne's *Essais*.

Chassignet, Jean-Baptiste (*c.* 1570-*c.* 1635): devotional poet.

Cholières, Nicolas de (1509-92): poet; wrote stories framed by conversations.

Clichtove, Josse van (1470-1543): reform-minded, Catholic, Flemish theologian, based in France.

Coras, Jean de (1513/14-1572): Protestant jurist; chronicled the famous Martin Guerre case of identity theft.

Corrozet, Gilles (1510-64): disseminated humanism in vernacular works including an antiquarian treatise on Paris.

Crenne, Helisenne de: *see* **Briet de Crenne**.

Crespin, Jean (*c.* 1520-72): printer; wrote the major Calvinist martyrology.

Cujas, Jacques (1522-90): humanist jurist; further developed Budé and Alciato's historicizing approach to Roman law.

Cymbalum mundi (1538): anonymous, enigmatic, philosophical dialogue (possibly by Des Périers); censured as heretical.

Daneau, Lambert (*c.* 1530-95): Protestant theologian.

D'Aubigné, Agrippa (1552-1630): militant Calvinist chronicler of recent traumatic history, in vivid verse and prose; also wrote love poetry and racy comic fiction.

Denisot, Nicolas (1515-59): poet; possibly wrote a prose romance (*L'Amant ressuscité*).

Des Autels, Guillaume (1529-1581): poet; wrote a prose romance imitating Rabelais.

Des Périers, Bonaventure (*c.* 1500-44): humanist; wrote a collection of novellas (and possibly the *Cymbalum mundi*).

Desportes, Philippe (1546-1623): poet of religion and love; rivalled Ronsard in popularity.

Des Roches, Catherine (1542-87): poet; hosted regular salon in Poitiers with her mother Madeleine.

Des Roches, Madeleine (*c.* 1520-87): poet.

Dolet, Étienne (1509-46): humanist, printer, translator, poet; promoted Ciceronianism; executed for heresy.

Dorat, Jean (1508-88): humanist poet and preceptor whose teaching fostered Pléiade poetry.

Du Bartas, Guillaume de Saluste (1544-90): Protestant whose philosophical and religious poetry, on an epic scale, was widely read, translated and imitated.

Du Bellay, Joachim (1522/25-1560): outstanding French, neo-Latin and Pléiade poet.

Duchesne, Joseph (*c.* 1544-1609): physician and philosophical poet.

Du Fail, Noël (*c.* 1520-91): wrote stories framed by conversations.

Du Guillet, Pernette (*c.* 1520-45): Lyon noblewoman whose extraordinary love poetry was published just after her death.

Du Haillan, Bernard de Girard (1535-1610): royal historiographer.

Du Monin, Jean-Édouard (1557-86): philosophical poet and dramatist.

Du Perron, Jacques Davy (1556-1618): Cardinal well known for his speeches, sermons and tracts.

Du Plessis-Mornay, Philippe (1549-1623): Protestant polemicist.

Du Vair, Guillaume (1556-1621): magistrate celebrated for political oratory; promoted neo-Stoicism.

Emilio, Paolo (?-1529): royal historiographer.

Estienne family: dynasty of humanist printers who also wrote. Both the Parisian polymath **Charles Estienne** (1504-1564) and his brother **Robert** (1503-59) produced pioneering dictionaries. Robert became a Protestant and relocated to Geneva, where his son **Henri** (1531-98) wrote important works ranging from satire to philology. Charles's Catholic daughter **Nicole** (1542/44-1584/96) wrote unpublished poems about married women's misery.

Fauchet, Claude (1530-1602): magistrate; wrote a Gallican, nationalistic, antiquarian history of France.

Fernel, Jean (1497-58): medical writer.

Fine, Oronce (1494-1555): humanist mathematician.

Flore, Jeanne: name under which a 1530 collection of stories was published.

Fontaine, Charles (1514-1564/70): Platonic poet.

Garnier, Robert (1544-90): prominent magistrate; the leading author of tragedies.

Gilles, Pierre (1490-1555): humanist topographer, natural historian.

Gohory, Jacques (1520-76): polymath, translator; promoted alchemy and Paracelsian medicine.

Goulart, Simon (1543-1628): Calvinist pastor, leader, author; translated, annotated and adapted numerous works, ancient and modern; wrote commentary on Du Bartas's *Sepmaine*.

Gournay, Marie de (1566-1645): writer on poetics, ethics, grammar, sex inequality; translator from ancient Latin; editor of Montaigne's *Essais*.

Grévin, Jacques (1538-70): poet, dramatist.

Gringore, Pierre (*c.* 1475-1538/39): *rhétoriqueur* poet.

Habert, François (*c.* 1508-61): translator and court poet.

Habert, Isaac (*c.* 1560-*c.* 1615): wrote philosophical and other poetry.

Héroet, Antoine (*c.* 1492-1568): Platonic poet.

Hervet, Gentien (1499-1584): anti-Protestant polemicist; humanist translator of ancient Greek works into Latin.

Hesteau de Nuisement, Clovis (*c.* 1550-?): poet of love and alchemy.

Hotman, François (1524-90): militant Calvinist jurist; wrote radically about the political structures France should have.

Jamyn, Amadis (*c.* 1540-93): poet; Ronsard's page then secretary.

Jodelle, Étienne (1532-73): Pléiade poet and dramatist.

Joubert, Laurent (1529-83): Protestant physician; works include treatises on laughter and on incorrect medical opinions.

Labé, Louise (*c.* 1520-66): Lyon author of distinctive love poetry and a prose debate about love; their publication was unprecedented for a *bourgeoise*.

La Boétie, Étienne de (1530-63): Catholic magistrate whose anti-tyranny treatise was published posthumously by

Protestants; Montaigne wrote powerfully about their friendship.

La Borderie, Bertrand de (1507/20-?): courtier whose text on the sexual politics of court life relaunched the *querelle des femmes.*

La Ceppède, Jean de (*c.* 1550-1622): devotional poet.

Lambin, Denis (1519-72): leading humanist scholar.

La Noue, François de (1531-91): Protestant soldier; wrote on political and military topics.

La Popelinière, Henri Lancelot Voisin de (1541-1608): chronicler of the Wars of Religion; Protestant, but pursued Bodin's ideal of impartial history writing.

La Primaudaye, Pierre de (1546-1619): Protestant; compiled an encyclopaedia.

Larivey, Pierre de (1540/41-1619): wrote comedies; translated Italian works.

La Taille, Jean de (1533/40-1611/12): wrote tragedies and comedies.

La Vigne, André de (*c.* 1470-after 1515): *rhétoriqueur* poet.

Lefèvre de la Boderie, Guy (1541-98): wrote philosophical and religious poetry, steeped in 'ancient theology'; translator.

Lefèvre d'Étaples, Jacques (?-1536): Aristotelian humanist, also drawn to Platonism and mysticism; central to reform-minded, Catholic evangelism.

Le Gendre, Marie: published prose reflections on moral topics (1584).

Le Loyer, Pierre (1550-1634): poet, demonologist.

Lemaire de Belges, Jean (*c.* 1473-*c.* 1515): outstanding *rhétoriqueur* poet.

Le Roy, Louis (*c.* 1510-77): wrote on the philosophy of history; translator, notably of Plato into French.

Léry, Jean de (1536-1613): Calvinist pastor; chronicled first-hand two traumatic events – Villegagnon's Brazil expedition and the Sancerre siege.

L'Estoile, Pierre de (1546-1611): kept a vast journal of current affairs, published posthumously.

Lucinge, René de (1553-1615): Savoyard soldier, diplomat; wrote on the life span of empires and the uses of history.

Magny, Olivier de (*c.* 1520-61): poet in the Pléiade orbit.

Marot, Clément (1496-1544): outstanding, best-selling poet whose work ranged from worldly to spiritual; accused of Lutheranism by traditional Catholics.

Marot, Jean (*c.* 1464-*c.* 1524): *rhétoriqueur* poet; father of Clément.

Marquets, Anne de (*c.* 1533-88): Dominican nun; devotional poet; translator.

Martin, Jean (*c.* 1507-*c.* 1553): translator into French of key Latin and Italian works.

Masson, Jean (1544-1611): erstwhile Jesuit; polymath, historian.

Matthieu, Pierre (1563-1621): Leaguer; royal historiographer.

Meigret, Louis (*c.* 1510-*c.* 1560): grammarian; tried to reform French orthography.

Monluc, Blaise de (*c.* 1499-77): Catholic soldier whose memoirs were published posthumously.

Montaigne, Michel de (1533-92): magistrate whose *Essais* inaugurated new models of subjectivity; also wrote a travel journal (published posthumously) and translated a theological treatise.

Montenay, Georgette de (1540-*c.* 1581): poet whose best-selling emblem book was in the Alciato tradition.

Montreux, Nicolas de (*c.* 1561-1608): wrote prose fiction, drama (notably pastoral), history and theology.

Muret, Marc-Antoine (1526-85): prestigious humanist teacher; works include drama and a commentary on Ronsard's *Amours.*

Navarre, Marguerite de (1492-1549): outstanding works infused with evangelical spirituality (some published only posthumously): drama, poetry, a collection of novellas. François Ier's sister.

Nicolai, Nicolas de (1517-83): soldier, spy; wrote chorography, on France and the Orient.

Olivétan (*c.* 1505-38): Protestant relative of Calvin; produced pioneering French translation of the Bible.

Olivier, Jean (?-1540): humanist bishop, translator, neo-Latin poet.

Palissy, Bernard (*c.* 1510-89): Calvinist artisan (potter and enameller) whose innovative publications on naturalist questions owe more to observation and experiment than to textual authorities.

Palma Cayet, Pierre-Victor (1525-1610): converted to Protestantism and then back again; wrote on oriental languages and recent history.

Paré, Ambroise (*c.* 1510-90): barber surgeon; published pioneering medical works.

Parthenay, Catherine de (1554-1631): varied writings, unpublished in her lifetime and long after.

Pasquier, Étienne (1529-1615): magistrate and *politique*; works include a vast history of French traditions and a best-selling collection of letters.

Passerat, Jean (1534-1602): humanist and poet.

Peletier du Mans, Jacques (1517-82): important philosophical and love poet; wrote prose on mathematics, astronomy, medicine and poetics; tried to reform French orthography.

Périon, Joachim (*c.* 1499-*c.* 1557): Benedictine, humanist; produced numerous editions and Latin translations of Greek texts, notably most of Aristotle.

Pibrac, Guy du Faur de (1529-84): leading magistrate; wrote poetry on country life and a best-selling collection of ethical four-liners ('moral quatrains').

Pins, Jean de (*c.* 1470-1537): humanist and diplomat.

Pithou, Pierre (1539-96): ex-Protestant jurist; a *Satyre Ménippée* contributor.

Poissenot, Bénigne (*c.* 1550-?): wrote innovative short stories.

Postel, Guillaume (1510-81): extraordinary polymath; pursued controversial paths of learning (including the Koran and the Jewish cabala), seeking common ground between religions.

Poupo, Pierre (*c.* 1552-*c.* 1592): Calvinist devotional poet.

Rabelais, François (1483/94-1553): physician, humanist scholar, ex-monk; his chronicles of the deeds of giants are among the greatest fictions ever written, combining satire, scatology, philosophy, humanism, evangelism and folklore.

Ramus (Pierre de la Ramée) (*c.* 1515-72): innovative Protestant philosopher; rejected scholasticism and Aristotle's authority; developed a new dialectic and method. Ramism thrived especially in Protestant countries.

Rapin, Nicolas (1539-1608): poet and translator.

Riolan, Jean (*c.* 1546-1606): orthodox professor of medicine.

Romieu, Marie de (*c.* 1545-?): poet and translator.

Rondelet, Guillaume (1507-66): physician and naturalist.

Ronsard, Pierre de (1524-85): prolific poet of enormous range and expressive power; wrote about love, the cosmos, nature, history, politics, religion, death and much else.

Sadolet, Jacques (Jacopo Sadoleto) (1476-1547): humanist and reforming bishop.

Sainte-Marthe, Scévole de (1536-1623): neo-Latin and French poet.

Saint-Gelais, Mellin de (1491-1558): court poet.

Salmon Macrin, Jean (1490-1557): outstanding neo-Latin poet.

Satyre Ménippée (1594): influential anti-League satire, composed collectively, published anonymously.

Scaliger, Joseph-Juste (1540-1609): outstanding humanist scholar; Protestant; son of Julius Caesar Scaliger.

Scaliger, Julius Caesar (1484-1558): humanist scholar whose Latin treatise on poetics promoted the shift to 'neo-classical' aesthetics characteristic of much seventeenth-century French writing.

Scève, Maurice (*c.* 1500-*c.* 1560): outstanding Lyon poet; wrote a love cycle and a poem describing humanity immediately after the Fall (*Microcosme*).

Sebillet, Thomas (1512-89): translator; wrote on French poetics.

Seyssel, Claude de (1450-1520): diplomat, bishop, pioneering vernacular translator of ancients (e.g. Herodotus, Thucydides); in a widely read treatise, advocated a constitutionalist (non-absolutist) theory of monarchy.

Sponde, Jean de (1557-95): humanist, translator and outstanding devotional poet.

Stuart, Mary (1542-87): Mary Queen of Scots; wrote French poetry.

Tabourot des Accords, Étienne (1549-90): poet, story-writer; collected verbal tricks and games.

Tahureau, Jacques (1527-55): poet in Pléiade orbit; wrote satirical prose dialogues.

Taillemont, Claude de (*c.*1506-?): Lyon poet.

Taillepied, Noël (*c.* 1540-89): polemicist friar.

Thevet, André (1516-92): royal cosmographer; central to cosmography's emergence in France.

Thou, Jacques-Auguste de (1553-1617): high-ranking magistrate; neo-Latin poet; his celebrated (Latin) history of recent times used the new, would-be impartial humanist historiography to promote *politique* tolerance.

Tory, Geoffroy (*c.* 1480-1533): humanist, printer and translator.

Turnèbe, Adrien (1512-65): leading humanist scholar.

Turnèbe, Odet de (1552-81): humanist and poet; wrote a comedy; son of Adrien.

Tyard, Pontus de (1521/22-1605): wrote metaphysically charged poetry and prose (mostly vernacular) – on topics ranging from love to astrology – imbued with philosophy (especially neo-Platonic) and, increasingly, religion.

Valois, Marguerite de (1553-1615): while her estranged husband became Henri IV and reigned, she wrote extraordinary memoirs, published posthumously.

Verville, François Béroalde de (1556-1626): ex-Protestant, cathedral canon and polymath; wrote numerous philosophical, poetical and fictional works before finishing with a scathing satire of literate culture.

Viète, François (1560-1603): pioneering mathematician.

Vigenère, Blaise de (1523-96): humanist, translator and occult philosopher.

Vigneulles, Philippe de (1471-1528): local historian and writer of novellas.

Vignier, Nicolas (1530-96): physician; ex-Protestant royal historiographer.

Viret, Pierre (1511-71): leader of the Lausanne Protestant Church; wrote especially dialogues.

Yver, Jacques (*c.* 1548-1571/72): wrote a widely read collection of novellas.

Index